"𝕰asy 𝕽eading 𝕺ld 𝖂orld 𝕷iterature"

𝕿welfth 𝕹ight

LEVEL 4

Series Designer
Philip J. Solimene

Editor
Laura Solimene

Cover Art by
Donald V. Lannon III

Black & White Illustrations by
Ken Landgraf

EDCON PUBLISHING

New York

Story Adaptor
Julianne Davidow

Author
William Shakespeare

About the Title

It is believed that William Shakespeare was
commissioned to write this amusing play for
the twelfth night of the Christmas Season, 1601.
Shakespeare did so, and named this play, *Twelfth
Night*, however, the title has nothing to
do with the play itself.

Copyright © 2004
A/V Concepts Corp.
info@edconpublishing.com
1-888-553-3266   Fax 1-888-518-1564
30 Montauk Blvd. Oakdale NY 11769
Portions of this book may be reproduced for classroom use.
All other rights reserved.
www.edconpublishing.com

Printed in U.S.A.
ISBN# 1-55576-347-2

CONTENTS

Interdisciplinary Teaching Suggestions........4
Words Used..5

No.	TITLE	SYNOPSIS	PAGE
31	**Arrival in Illyria**	Viola's ship has sunk, but she arrives safely in an ancient, old city. She is very sad, for she fears her twin brother has drowned.	6
32	**Falling in Love**	Viola, dressed as a man (Cesario), quickly becomes the Duke's favorite servant. Sent to Olivia's to tell her of his master's love, Olivia begins to have feelings for Cesario.	12
33	**Comings and Goings**	Viola's twin brother arrives in Illyria. He had not drowned after all. Maria comes up with an idea to get back at Malvolio for being so mean.	18
34	**Secrets and Tricks**	Cesario (Viola) wishes she could tell the Duke that she is a woman and that she loves him. Maria's letter has Malvolio convinced that Olivia loves him.	24
35	**Pretending Brings Trouble**	Olivia, not knowing Cesario is really a woman, tells Cesario that she loves him.	30
36	**Malvolio is Made the Fool**	Olivia thinks Malvolio is going mad and has him locked away in a room.	36
37	**Drawing Swords**	Cesario (Viola) is very frightened at the thought of taking part in a duel. Antonio arrives just in time to stop the duel, but he is arrested.	42
38	**The Struggle**	Andrew, thinking Sebastian to be Cesario, fights with him. Olivia, thinking Sebastian to be Cesario, calls him her dear, sweet friend. Sebastian thinks these people are mad.	48
39	**Help is on the Way**	Maria, Toby, and Feste have fun at Malvolio's expense. Olivia asks Sebastian to be her husband.	54
40	**Brother Finds Sister**	The Duke thinks Cesario has deceived him. When Sebastian appears in the garden, Viola shakes off her disguise and begins to tell her story.	60

Comprehension Check Answer Key..........................67
Vocabulary Check Answer Key................................69

About the Author

William Shakespeare was born in 1564, in Stratford-on-Avon, a city in England. His mother's name was Mary Arden. His father, John, was a wealthy businessman. There is very little known about William Shakespeare's early life. It is believed that he attended a local grammar school where the students learned Latin, public speaking, and religion. Shakespeare married Anne Hathaway in 1582. They had three children. Susanna was first, followed by twins Hamnet, and Judith. In 1584, Shakespeare left Stratford and went to London.

By 1592, Shakespeare was a well-known actor and playwright. In 1599, Shakespeare, along with others, opened the Globe Theatre. In the early 1600's, Shakespeare's company worked under King James I and became known as the King's Men. In 1608, the King's Men acquired the Blackfriars Theatre, which became their winter home. In 1613, the Globe was destroyed by fire and was rebuilt a year later. However, by that time, Shakespeare had retired from writing. Shakespeare died in his hometown of Stratford on April 23, 1616.

Interdisciplinary Teaching Suggestions

Language Arts:
Build a Theatre: In 1599, the Globe Theatre was built in Southwark, London, where Shakespeare's plays were performed. Research and construct the Globe Theatre.
Create a Picture Book: Have each student select a character from the story and create their own picture book based on their character's journey in the story.

Math:
Compare Prices: What was the average cost of food, shelter, and clothing in Shakespeare's day? How were goods and services paid for?

Science:
Study Earthquakes: During Shakespeare's life, there was an earthquake in London. What causes earthquakes? What was the effect of this event on London?

Social Studies:
Compare Lifestyles: During Shakespeare's life, in 1607, the first English settlement was established in Jamestown, Virginia. Research and compare life in Jamestown and life in London during Shakespeare's time. Create models of each society.

Geography:
Create a Map: This play opens in the country of Illyria, a place we now call Yugoslavia. Break students up into two groups. Have one group research and create a map of ancient Europe. Have the other group create a map of Europe today.

General:
Create a Classroom Bulletin Board: Divide students into small groups. Make each group responsible for an area of the bulletin board that pertains to the story. Create a story cluster describing literary elements from the story, for example: setting, characters, and plot.

WORDS USED

Story 31	Story 32	Story 33	Story 34	Story 35

KEY WORDS

Story 31	Story 32	Story 33	Story 34	Story 35
coin	burst	companion	accept	admire
helpful	entire/entirely	couple	command	although
instrument	favorite	flute	crouch	bet
mast	gentleman	fond	disappointment	coax
music	jealous	midnight	seal	dull
shone	manners	sight	stocking	God

NECESSARY WORDS

Story 31	Story 32	Story 33	Story 34	Story 35
court	cruel	challenge	convince	behalf
death	echo	duel	hedge	excellent
desire	lord	farewell	pain	madam
duke	mourn	meanwhile	rascal	niece
musician	soul	stomach		pity
servant	veil	stoop/stooped		recently

Story 36	Story 37	Story 38	Story 39	Story 40

KEY WORDS

Story 36	Story 37	Story 38	Story 39	Story 40
arrest	contain	ache	breath/breathed	especially
explore	dignity	mystery	fortunate	explanation
grateful	habit	nuisance	imitate	favor
hadn't	lad	quit	ink	opposite
port	thankful	remove	nonsense	service
property	treat	shoulder	robin	whom

NECESSARY WORDS

Story 36	Story 37	Story 38	Story 39	Story 40
devil	enemy/enemies	agree	fake	deceive
entertain	escort	dagger	ignorance	praise
nervous	offend	realize	minister	vow
prayers	officer		peace	
sensible	sword		priest	

Arrival in Illyria

PREPARATION

Key Words

coin   (koin)   metal money
I found a shiny <u>coin</u> in the street.

helpful   (help´ fəl)   giving help; useful
Maria thought it would be <u>helpful</u> if she set the table for dinner.

instrument   (in´ strə mənt) a thing used to make music
After practicing on the violin, Ray put his <u>instrument</u> away in its case.

mast   (mast)   a long pole of wood or metal set upright on a ship to support the sails and rigging (ropes, chains, etc.)
Sally spotted the tall <u>mast</u> of the ship with its sails flapping in the breeze.

music   (mū´ zik)   sounds that are pleasing or beautiful to hear
The dancer moved beautifully to the <u>music</u> of the band.

shone   (shōn)   shined; glistened; sparkled
The sun <u>shone</u> brightly on the river.

Arrival in Illyria

Necessary Words

court   (kôrt)   pay loving attention to; to date; woo
The young man will <u>court</u> the girl by bringing her flowers every day.

death   (deth)   the act or fact of dying; the ending of life
The old man's <u>death</u> was calm and peaceful.

desire   (di zīr´)   strong wish; want
Cathy had a <u>desire</u> to travel to other countries.

duke   (dük)   a nobleman of the highest title, just below a prince
The <u>duke</u> ruled his country fairly and had no enemies.

musician   (mū zish´ən) someone skilled in music who sings or plays an instrument
Lenny is a <u>musician</u> who plays the piano.

servant   (sėr´ vənt)   a person who waits on and works for another
The <u>servant</u> brought the king his dinner.

People, Places

Illyria   is an ancient (old) country taken over by the Romans in 35-33 B.C. Illyria was just across from Italy.

Sir Andrew   is a friend of Olivia's uncle. He is trying to court Olivia.

Arrival in Illyria

All the Duke can think about is the beautiful Olivia.

Preview: 1. Read the name of the story.
2. Look at the picture.
3. Read the sentence under the picture.
4. Read the first four paragraphs of the story.
5. Then answer the following question.

You learned from your preview that the music made Duke Orsino think about
    ____a. his servant, Curio.
    ____b. hunting for deer.
    ____c. his desire to play an instrument.
    ____d. Olivia.

Turn to the Comprehension Check on page 10 for the right answer.

Now read the story.
Read to find out why Viola dresses as a man.

Arrival in Illyria

"If music be the food of love, play on," said Duke Orsino. He was in his palace, dreaming of Olivia. His musicians were playing their instruments.

"If I hear enough music, maybe I will grow sick of it. Maybe my desire for it will go away. Stop!" said the Duke to his musicians. "No more. Put down your instruments!"

"Will you not go with me to hunt deer today?" asked his servant Curio. He wanted to cheer up his master. The Duke seemed to be very sad.

"All I can think about is the beautiful Olivia," said Orsino. He put his hand on his heart. "When I first saw her, I became as gentle as a deer. Now I don't want to hunt those animals any more."

Just then Valentine, another servant, came in. The Duke had sent him to Olivia's house to find out if she would meet with him.

"What did Olivia say?" Orsino asked him.

"I did not see her," said Valentine. "Her servant told me that Olivia will see no man for seven years. She is full of sadness over her brother's death."

Orsino leaned back in his chair and his eyes shone with tears. "Poor, sweet Olivia," he cried. "How I do desire to court her."

Orsino didn't know then that someone had just come to his country by chance---someone who would prove to be helpful to him. A young woman named Viola had just arrived in Illyria. She stood on the shore, looking out to sea. The late-day sun shone on the waves. Her ship had sunk, and she and the captain were saved. But her twin brother was lost.

"What is this country?" Viola asked the Captain.

"This is Illyria, my lady," he said.

"Oh, my poor brother must be in heaven. But perhaps he did not drown after all?"

The Captain put his hand on her arm. "Let me make you feel better. I know I saw your brother. He had tied himself to a mast that was floating in the water."

"Thank you for telling me that," Viola said, putting a gold coin in his hand. "Now I have hope. May that mast be a strong one!

"You seem to know this country," she said to the Captain. "Who rules here?"

"Yes, I know this place well," he said, "for I was born not far from here. The ruler is a duke by the name of Orsino."

"I have heard my father speak of him. Is he still without a wife?"

"Yes, but it is known that he wants to win the love of the fair Olivia. Her father was a count who died a year ago. And now, her brother has died as well. She'll see no man because of her sadness."

It is not good for a woman to be alone in a strange land, thought Viola. *If only I could hide myself for a time.* Then she had an idea. "I would like to meet that lady," Viola said to the Captain. "Will you take me to her?"

"The lady will see no one, I'm afraid---not even the Duke!"

"Then will you help me dress in man's clothes so that I may serve the Duke? I will pay you well with more gold coins. I cannot tell you why just now. But I will make myself helpful to him. Can you keep my secret?"

"Yes, my lady. I promise not to say a word."

I will call myself Cesario, she thought.

And so Viola started out on her adventure to help the Duke.

*   *   *

While the Duke dreamed of Olivia, and Viola was dressing as a man, much was happening at Olivia's house. The Duke wasn't the only one in love with the fair lady.

"Olivia said you brought a foolish knight to court her," said Maria, Olivia's servant, to Sir Toby Belch.

"I'm her uncle and I can do as I please," he replied. "She's taking her brother's death too hard. It's not healthy."

Maria shot Sir Toby an unkind look. "I can see you do as *you* please---you and Sir Andrew! He has been with us too long. All you two do is drink and make merry," she said.

"Sir Andrew is a rich man and can play lovely music," replied Toby.

"He is a fool who will spend all his money," answered Maria.

Just then, Sir Andrew walked in the door. "I'm going home tomorrow," he said sadly. "Olivia does not want to spend time with me. Duke Orsino has a better chance than I."

"She will have nothing to do with him!" said Sir Toby. "You still have a chance. Stay, and I will help you." Then he had an idea. "Tell me Andrew, how good can you dance?"

"I'm quite light on my feet," he answered.

Sir Toby smiled. "Let's go my friend. We have work to do."

Arrival in Illyria

COMPREHENSION CHECK

Choose the best answer.

Preview Answer:
d. Olivia.

1. At the beginning of this story, what made the Duke very sad?
   ____a. Music
   ____b. He had lost his desire to hunt deer.
   ____c. His desire for Olivia was not being satisfied.
   ____d. He was becoming too gentle with everyone.

2. Who asked Duke Orsino to go deer hunting?
   ____a. Valentine
   ____b. Curio
   ____c. Sir Toby Belch
   ____d. Sir Andrew

3. Olivia would see no man for seven years because
   ____a. she had to finish school first.
   ____b. she was too young to be seen with a man.
   ____c. she was full of sadness over the deaths of her father and brother.
   ____d. she was full of sadness over her mother's death.

4. Viola had come to Illyria by way of
   ____a. shipwreck.
   ____b. her brother's fishing boat.
   ____c. horse and wagon.
   ____d. airplane.

5. Like Olivia, Viola
   ____a. was beautiful.
   ____b. was sweet.
   ____c. wanted nothing to do with men.
   ____d. had just lost a brother.

6. Viola decides to dress like a man because
   ____a. she wants to meet Olivia.
   ____b. she knows it's not good for a woman to be alone in a strange land.
   ____c. she wants to serve the Duke.
   ____d. she wants to be like her brother.

7. Viola dresses as a man and calls herself
   ____a. Cesario.
   ____b. Caesar.
   ____c. Cyrano.
   ____d. Claudius.

8. Sir Toby Belch feels that Olivia
   ____a. is not healthy.
   ____b. spends too much money.
   ____c. is taking her brother's death too hard.
   ____d. is a foolish young woman.

9. Another name for this story could be
   ____a. "Foolish Knights."
   ____b. "Olivia, the Beautiful."
   ____c. "A Rich Man Named Andrew."
   ____d. "Viola's Adventure."

10. This story is mainly about
    ____a. why Duke Orsino was very sad.
    ____b. how Viola's brother was lost at sea.
    ____c. how Olivia lost her brother.
    ____d. how Viola and the captain had come to find themselves in a strange land.

Check your answers with the Key on page 67.

This page may be reproduced for classroom use.

Arrival in Illyria

VOCABULARY CHECK

coin	helpful	instrument	mast	music	shone

I. Sentences to Finish
Fill in the blank in each sentence with the correct key word from the box above.

1. Charlie plays an _____called a flute.

2. Charlie plays lovely _____on his flute.

3. The car's headlights _____in the deer's face and frightened the animal.

4. I threw a _____into the wishing well and made a wish.

5. "It would be _____if you would pick up after yourself," said Mother.

6. As the ship began to sink, the captain held onto the ship's _____with all his might.

II. Matching
Write the letter of the correct meaning from Column B next to the key word in Column A.

Column A	Column B
____1. instrument	a. a long pole of wood or metal that supports a ship's sails
____2. shone	b. metal money
____3. helpful	c. shined; glistened; sparkled
____4. coin	d. giving help; useful
____5. mast	e. a thing used to make music
____6. music	f. sounds that are pleasing or beautiful to hear

Check your answers with the Key on page 69.

This page may be reproduced for classroom use.

Falling in Love

PREPARATION

Key Words

burst	(bėrst)	go, come, do, etc. by force or suddenly *"Don't <u>burst</u> into my room without knocking,"* *said Pam to her little sister.*
entire **entirely**	(en tīr´) (en tīr´ lē)	whole; complete wholly; fully *It took Dad the <u>entire</u> day to clean out the garage.* *"I agree with you <u>entirely</u>," said Mother to Aunt Jane.*
favorite	(fā´ vər it)	best liked; liked better than others *What is your <u>favorite</u> flower?* *What is your <u>favorite</u> candy?*
gentleman	(jen´ tl mən)	a man with good manners *A <u>gentleman</u> would not push into line ahead of others.*
jealous	(jel´ əs)	to be afraid that someone you love may love or like someone else better *The child was <u>jealous</u> when anyone played with the new baby.*
manners	(man´ ərs)	polite ways of behaving *People with <u>manners</u> say, "Please" and "Thank You."*

Falling in Love

Necessary Words

cruel (krü´ əl)   ready to hurt others or feel joy when they are sad
> *The cruel master worked his men all day without food.*
> *The cruel man left his dog outside in the freezing rain.*

echo (ek´ ō)   sounding again; the repeat of a sound; you hear an echo when a sound you make bounces back from a far-away hill or wall so that you hear it again
> *When Sarah couldn't find Billy in the cave, she called his name. But all she heard was the echo of her own voice.*

lord (lôrd)   ruler; master; someone who has power
> *The servant tried hard to please his lord.*

mourn (môrn)   to be very sad or sorrowful over someone's death
> *Time is a great healer for those who mourn.*
> *Jason mourned the death of his dog.*

soul (sōl)   the part of a person that is spirit; some people believe that the soul never dies
> *John's mother told him that his dead grandfather's soul was in heaven.*

veil (vāl)   a piece of very thin cloth worn to hide the face
> *The woman wore a veil so she wouldn't be recognized.*

Falling in Love

The Duke tells Cesario to go to Olivia's home and speak for him.
"Pretend that you are me," he says. "Say the words that will make her mine."

Preview: 1. Read the name of the story.
2. Look at the picture.
3. Read the sentences under the picture.
4. Read the first five paragraphs of the story.
5. Then answer the following question.

You learned from your preview that Cesario
____a. could not keep a secret.
____b. could not be trusted.
____c. had been at court for three months.
____d. was the Duke's favorite servant.

Turn to the Comprehension Check on page 16 for the right answer.

Now read the story.
Read to find out what Olivia thinks of Cesario when they first meet.

Falling in Love

"You've only been at court for three days, Cesario," said Valentine. "And already the Duke trusts you."

Viola was dressed as a man. Everybody at Duke Orsino's court knew her as Cesario.

"Where is Cesario?" said the Duke, as he burst in the room. The entire room was full of servants.

Cesario came forward.

The Duke went quickly over to his favorite new servant. He took Cesario aside. "Cesario, you know my secret. I want Olivia as my wife. Go to her home and talk to her. Pretend that you are me. Say the words that will make her mine."

"But my lord, people say she is very sad and sees no one. She will never let me in."

The Duke walked up and down the room, his hands behind his back.

"If you are calm and say you will not leave, she will see you," the Duke said finally.

"What would you have me tell her, my lord?" asked Cesario.

"Tell her you speak for me. You are young and very good looking. And your voice is soft like a woman's. She will surely listen to you. I will reward you with many gold coins - my fortune will be your fortune!"

Oh, this is hard, thought Viola, *for I have fallen in love with Orsino. How I wish that he could love me, and not Olivia. But he thinks I'm a man. He doesn't know that I'm really a woman.*

And so, with a heavy heart, Viola made her way to Olivia's house. At the same time, Olivia's Fool, Feste, talked with his lady.

"Dear lady, why do you mourn so?" asked Feste.

"You know I mourn for my dead brother," said Olivia, wiping her eyes.

"But my lady, his soul has already gone to heaven."

"I know his soul is in heaven, Fool," said Olivia, making her way over to the window. She looked out at the garden. It was there that she and her brother had played as children.

"Then you are a fool to mourn for a soul that is gone," said Feste.

Just then Olivia's servant, Malvolio appeared. He was a man of few words. "A young man has come from Duke Orsino's court. He wishes to speak with you, my lady."

"What is he like?" asked Olivia, with interest. She had become less sad because of what Feste had said.

"He is young and good looking," replied Malvolio. "But he has bad manners and refuses to go away," he said sharply. Malvolio was jealous of any man who showed an interest in his lady.

Olivia had heard about this good-looking young man. "Tell him to wait," she told Malvolio. "And ask Maria to come to me," she said.

A few minutes later, Maria came before Olivia. "Malvolio said you wanted to see me, my lady. He didn't look happy."

"He's never happy," said Olivia. "Pay him no mind."

"I never do," answered Maria. "Now what can I do for my lady?"

"I need you to bring me a black veil," answered Olivia.

When Maria returned with the veil, Olivia covered her entire face with it. *I do not know this man*, thought Olivia. *Let him not know me too quickly.*

With her face entirely covered, Olivia asked Maria to let Cesario in.

"I have come from Duke Orsino," said Cesario with a bow. "Which of you is the lady of the house? Only the lady Olivia may hear my lord's message."

Olivia was taken with the young man's good looks. She turned to Maria. "You may go now," she said.

"Why have you come here?" asked Olivia, when they were alone.

"Will you not let me see your face?" asked Cesario.

"Why, of course," said Olivia, knowing he would be pleased with her looks. "Let me open the curtain and show you the entire picture," said Olivia, as she took off her veil.

"'It would be cruel not to marry and have a child, so the world could have a copy of such beauty,' my lord and master would say. You know the Duke is in love with you."

"Your lord already knows I cannot love *him*," replied Olivia.

"If I were my lord, I would shout your name to the hills until I heard the echo, 'Olivia!' Then you might know how much I love you."

This man is very sweet, thought Olivia. *I really like him.* "You speak like a real gentleman," said Olivia.

"I am a gentleman," said Cesario, "but I'm also a lowly servant who has come to tell you of my master's love."

Olivia looked Cesario up and down. "Tell your lord I cannot love him. But you may come to me again and tell me how he takes it." She handed Cesario some gold coins. "Here, this is for you," she said.

"Keep your coins, for I will not take your tip," said Cesario. "Good-by cruel lady."

After Cesario left, Olivia thought, *If only his master was this man! His voice, his face, his manners, please me. I must let him know my feelings. I'll pretend he left a ring with me and give him my own favorite ring.* Then she called for Malvolio.

Malvolio burst into the room. He'd been jealously waiting outside.

"Go run after the gentleman who was just here. He left a ring with me." She handed Malvolio a gold ring. "Give this to him. Tell him to return to me tomorrow."

After Malvolio left, Olivia sat thinking. *How could I fall in love so quickly? But I could not help myself. His words echo in my mind. Whatever will be will be.*

Falling in Love

COMPREHENSION CHECK

Choose the best answer.

1. Cesario had been at court for only _____ days, yet he was already the Duke's favorite servant.
   ____a. two
   ____b. seven
   ____c. three
   ____d. ten

2. The Duke wanted Cesario to go to Olivia and
   ____a. speak for him.
   ____b. mourn for him.
   ____c. tell her a secret.
   ____d. shake some sense into her.

3. The Duke thought Cesario
   ____a. was full of wisdom.
   ____b. was someone he could trust.
   ____c. was a jerk.
   ____d. would make a good husband for Olivia.

4. Duke Orsino thinks Olivia will listen to Cesario because
   ____a. he is young.
   ____b. he is good looking.
   ____c. he has a soft voice.
   ____d. all of the above. (a, b, c.)

5. The Duke will make Cesario rich if Olivia
   ____a. will stop mourning her brother.
   ____b. will marry Cesario.
   ____c. will agree to marry him.
   ____d. will get rid of Feste.

6. Olivia went from "sad" to "almost glad" when
   ____a. Malvolio told her a young man from the Duke's court wished to speak with her.
   ____b. Feste told her that her brother's soul was in heaven.
   ____c. Cesario asked to see her face.
   ____d. Cesario refused to take her gold coins.

7. Malvolio loved
   ____a. Maria.
   ____b. Olivia.
   ____c. causing trouble.
   ____d. talking with anyone who would listen.

8. Olivia doesn't know it just yet, but she has just fallen in love with
   ____a. a servant.
   ____b. a young woman.
   ____c. a gentle man.
   ____d. a cruel lady.

9. Another name for this story could be
   ____a. "The Great Pretender."
   ____b. "A Day of Mourning."
   ____c. "The Black Veil."
   ____d. "Viola's Heavy Heart."

10. This story is mainly about
    ____a. Malvolio's jealousy.
    ____b. why the Duke puts his trust in Cesario.
    ____c. why Olivia is so sad.
    ____d. how Olivia came to fall in love with a woman.

Check your answers with the Key on page 67.

This page may be reproduced for classroom use.

falling in Love

VOCABULARY CHECK

burst	entire	favorite	gentleman	jealous	manners

I. Sentences to Finish
Fill in the blank in each sentence with the correct key word from the box above.

1. "Mind your _____," Mom said to Jim, as he reached across the table for the bread.

2. Elsa was so _____, she wouldn't let her husband dance with her sister.

3. When the sun _____ through the clouds, we headed back to the beach.

4. When my car broke down, a kind _____ offered to give me a lift home.

5. Spring is my _____ time of year.

6. The _____ class laughed when Jody's cat crawled out of her back-pack.

II. Making Sense of Sentences
Put a check next to YES if the sentence makes sense. Put a check next to NO if the sentence does not make sense.

1. Sally became *jealous* when her husband bought her a new car.   ___YES   ___NO

2. Billy hates to watch his *favorite* T.V. show.   ___YES   ___NO

3. We were amazed that Bob could eat the *entire* cake.   ___YES   ___NO

4. Carrie *burst* her hair every night before going to bed.   ___YES   ___NO

5. My brother Jeff has very poor table *manners.*   ___YES   ___NO

6. A *gentleman* is often unkind to others.   ___YES   ___NO

Check your answers with the Key on page 69.

This page may be reproduced for classroom use.

Comings and Goings

PREPARATION

Key Words

companion (kəm pan´yən) someone who shares in what another is doing
Every day, Sue and her <u>companion</u>, Mary, walk to school together.

couple (kup´l) two things that are the same or go together in some way; two of something; pair
I bought a <u>couple</u> of new tires for my bike.
I bought a <u>couple</u> of tickets to the game.

flute (flüt) a long, slender, pipe-like musical instrument that's played by blowing across a hole on one end
Harry played the <u>flute</u> in the school's band.

fond (fond) 1. loving
Jeannie gave her child a <u>fond</u> look.
2. to be fond of something means you like it very much
George has always been <u>fond</u> of music.

midnight (mid´nīt´) 12 o'clock at night; the middle of the night
Cinderella had to be home by <u>midnight</u>.

sight (sīt) to get or catch a view of something
After being at sea for several months, land was a welcome <u>sight</u>.

Comings and Goings

Necessary Words

challenge   (chal´ ənj)   a call or invitation to a game or contest
The blue team accepted the red team's <u>challenge</u>.

duel   (dü əl)   a fight between two people using guns, swords, or some other weapon
The <u>duel</u> between the lord and his servant ended with the servant's death.

farewell   (fãr´ wel´)   good wishes when saying good-by
Jim shouted, "<u>farewell</u>" to Bob, as Bob's ship pulled out of the harbor.

meanwhile   (mēn´ hwīl´)   1. in the time between
I have to leave for work in an hour; <u>meanwhile</u>, I'm going to rest.
2. at the same time
Dad cut the lawn; <u>meanwhile</u>, Rob bagged the grass cuttings.

stomach   (stum´ ək)   the part of the body that receives the food we eat
Sarah's <u>stomach</u> was full. She couldn't finish her dinner.

stoop   (stüp)   bend forward
stooped   *When the lady dropped her glove, the gentleman <u>stooped</u> down and picked it up.*

Comings and Goings

Antonio points the way to the Duke's court.

Preview: 1. Read the name of the story.
2. Look at the picture.
3. Read the sentence under the picture.
4. Read the first six paragraphs of the story.
5. Then answer the following question.

You learned from your preview that Antonio
_____a. saved Viola's life.
_____b. saved Sebastian's life.
_____c. had once saved the Duke's life.
_____d. almost drowned.

Turn to the Comprehension Check on page 22 for the right answer.

Now read the story.
Read to find out about the trick Maria will play on Malvolio.

Comings and Goings

A couple of men walked away from the shore. They were on another part of the coast from where Viola had arrived. One was a handsome young man named Sebastian. He looked exactly like Viola.

"My twin sister, Viola, must have drowned," said Sebastian. "I loved her so much that I wish I could have died *with* her."

His companion was a sea captain named Antonio. Antonio's ship had been sailing near Sebastian's, when he saw it crash against the rocks. When the ship began to sink, he quickly jumped into the water and saved Sebastian. But he never even saw Viola.

"Duke Orsino rules this land," said Antonio. "Let me show you around. I will be your companion."

"I can never thank you enough for saving my life," replied Sebastian. "But I do not wish to trouble you. My father knows the Duke, so I will go see him."

"Oh . . . , I must not go *there*. My ship was once in a fight with one of the Duke's ships," said Antonio. "I wish you a fond farewell, my friend," he said, pointing the way to the Duke's court.

"Farewell, Antonio," said Sebastian. "And again, I thank you for my life."

As Antonio began walking away, he had a sudden thought. *I may be in danger, but I must see that no harm comes to my friend. I have grown so very fond of him.* So when Sebastian was out of sight, Antonio followed him.

Meanwhile, Cesario (Viola) had left Olivia's house. Malvolio was soon chasing after him. In a couple of minutes he caught sight of Cesario and ran to meet him. "My lady said you left this ring with her, and she asked me to return it to you," said Malvolio.

"I left no ring with your lady," said Cesario. "What is this really about?"

"If my lady said you left it, then you left it," replied Malvolio, in an angry voice. Then he threw the ring at Cesario's feet. "Now you can stoop for it," he said, as he ran off.

Oh no! thought Viola. *Why would Olivia make this up? She must like me. Time must untie this knot, for it is too hard a knot for me to untie! The Duke loves Olivia and I, poor thing, love him! But to the Duke, I'm just a man. And Olivia likes me - a woman! What will I do?*

Viola stooped down and picked up the ring. Then she headed for Orsino's court.

*   *   *

It was after midnight at Olivia's house, and Sir Toby and Andrew were having a party. Feste the clown was playing the flute.

"It is past midnight and we should be in bed," said Andrew, his long, thin body stretched out in a chair.

"If it's midnight," replied Sir Toby, "then the night is still young." He rubbed his big, fat stomach and laughed. He was having a good time eating and drinking and didn't want the party to end. "Maria," he called, "bring us something to drink!"

As Maria prepared the drinks, Sir Toby danced to the tune of Feste's flute. When Maria returned, she laughed at how silly he looked. "Quiet! I think I hear Malvolio coming," said Maria. "He's sure to have you put out!"

Just then Malvolio entered wearing a nightcap and robe, and carrying a candle. "Don't you two know how late it is?" he cried. "Other people can't sleep with all your noisemaking!"

"Go hang yourself!" said Sir Toby, laughing so much, his big stomach was shaking.

Malvolio's blood boiled. "Sir Toby, my lady said that even though you are her uncle, you cannot live here if you keep behaving this way. She will hear about *this*!" he said, leaving in a hurry.

"Go shake your donkey's ears," said Maria, after he was gone.

"I should challenge him to a duel and then not show up," said Andrew. "That would make a fool of him!"

"I'll arrange it for you!" said Sir Toby, with excitement in his voice.

"You can challenge him later," said Maria. "I have a much better idea. I'll trick Malvolio and bring him down from his high horse! He thinks so much of himself! The foolish man tries to echo the speech and manners of a gentleman. I'll drop a letter in his path. He will read of Olivia's love for him. I can make my handwriting look just like my lady's. He'll think the letter was written by her! Just imagine the fun we'll have with *that!*"

"*Wonderful* idea," said Sir Toby, smiling at Andrew.

Maria was getting very sleepy. "Good night, friends," she said, "and pleasant dreams. Dream of the fun we'll have with Malvolio." Then she went off to bed.

"You'd better send for some more money, Andrew," said Sir Toby. "You'll win Olivia in the end. But meanwhile, we need to have a good time!"

Comings and Goings

COMPREHENSION CHECK

Choose the best answer.

1. Sebastian
   ____a. was angry with Antonio for not saving his sister.
   ____b. could never thank Antonio enough for saving his life.
   ____c. thought Antonio was a lot of trouble.
   ____d. thought Antonio would make a fine companion.

2. Antonio had grown _____ of Sebastian.
   ____a. tired
   ____b. sick
   ____c. fond
   ____d. fearful

3. Malvolio chased after Cesario to return a _____ he had left at Olivia's.
   ____a. key
   ____b. card
   ____c. glove
   ____d. ring

4. What is the "knot" that Viola hopes time will untie?
   ____a. Her "disguise" has kept her from winning the man she loves, and causes a woman to fall in love with her.
   ____b. The knot in her stomach
   ____c. The knot in her shoelaces
   ____d. The knot in her hair

5. Malvolio
   ____a. was not well liked.
   ____b. was always clowning around.
   ____c. was always getting into trouble.
   ____d. drank too much.

6. What had awakened Malvolio in the middle of the night?
   ____a. An alarm clock
   ____b. The sound of a flute
   ____c. The noise being made by Sir Toby, Andrew, and Feste
   ____d. Maria's loud voice

7. Malvolio would tell Olivia about the party, hoping she would
   ____a. fire Maria.
   ____b. ask Sir Toby to leave her house.
   ____c. join in the fun.
   ____d. give him a day off.

8. First, Sir Toby called for Maria to bring more drinks. Then, Malvolio appeared and ordered them to be quiet. Next,
   ____a. Maria went to bed.
   ____b. Feste left the party.
   ____c. Andrew challenged Malvolio to a duel.
   ____d. Maria came up with an idea that would make Malvolio look like a fool.

9. Another name for this story could be
   ____a. "Viola's Knot."
   ____b. "Olivia Returns Cesario's Ring."
   ____c. "The Party."
   ____d. "Maria's Trick."

10. This story is mainly about
   ____a. Malvolio's jealousy.
   ____b. how Viola's lie made life more difficult for her and those around her.
   ____c. why Antonio wouldn't go to the Duke's court.
   ____d. Sir Toby's midnight party.

Check your answers with the Key on page 67.

Comings and Goings

VOCABULARY CHECK

companion	couple	flute	fond	midnight	sight

I. Sentences to Finish
Fill in the blank in each sentence with the correct key word from the box above.

1. Hal's party ended at _____.

2. The _____ of her son's ship leaving the harbor, made Mrs. Jones cry.

3. Grandma has always been _____ of jelly donuts. They're her favorite!

4. Josh plays the drums. His brother plays the _____.

5. Lucy and her _____, Joe, go out to eat every Saturday night.

6. "May I fix you a _____ of eggs for breakfast?" asked Mother.

II. Using the Words
On the lines below, write six of your own sentences using the key words from the box above. Use each word once, and put a circle around the key word.

1._____

2._____

3._____

4._____

5._____

6._____

Check your answers with the Key on page 69.

This page may be reproduced for classroom use.

Secrets and Tricks

PREPARATION

Key Words

accept	(ak sept´)	1. to say "yes" to an offer *John asked Sally to marry him and she said she would* <u>accept</u>. 2. agree about something *The teacher could not* <u>accept</u> *Bill's answer as correct.*
command	(kə mand´)	give an order to; direct *As King, I* <u>command</u> *you to put down your sword.*
crouch	(krouch)	to stoop low with bent legs *When children get too close to the cat, he will* <u>crouch</u> *in a corner.*
disappointment	(dis´ ə point´ mənt)	the feeling you have when you don't get what you hoped for *When Tony didn't get the new bike he wanted for his birthday, his* <u>disappointment</u> *showed on his face.*
seal	(sēl)	a design pressed into wax and made into a stamp to show ownership *The queen placed her* <u>seal</u> *on all her letters.*
stocking	(stok´ ing)	a close-fitting, knitted covering of wool, cotton, or silk for the foot and leg *Frank wears woolen* <u>stockings</u> *during the winter.*

Secrets and Tricks

Necessary Words

convince   (kən vins´)   to cause someone to believe in something
Mary tried to <u>convince</u> her parents that she was old enough to go on a date.

hedge   (hej)   a thick row of bushes or small trees
Jim planted a <u>hedge</u> in front of his house.

pain   (pān)   the feeling of being hurt very much
The death of someone we love causes <u>pain</u>.

rascal   (ras´ kl)   1. a bad person who likes to make trouble
Bill wanted to know the name of the <u>rascal</u> who cut the tires on his car.
2. one who is full of mischief; naughty
"That little <u>rascal</u> down the street just rang my bell and ran away!"

Secrets and Tricks

The Duke asks Cesario if he likes the tune his musicians are playing.
"It truly echoes what the heart feels," answers Cesario.

Preview: 1. Read the name of the story.
2. Look at the picture.
3. Read the sentences under the picture.
4. Read the first six paragraphs of the story.
5. Then answer the following question.

You learned from your preview that the Duke was disappointed that
_____a. Cesario did not know how to sing.
_____b. Feste was not around to sing the song he wanted to
          hear.
_____c. Curio could not find Feste.
_____d. his musicians would not play his song.

Turn to the Comprehension Check on page 28 for the right answer.

Now read the story.
Read to find out how Malvolio is set up to look like a fool.

Secrets and Tricks

"Play some music," said Orsino to his musicians one morning. "I want to hear that old, sweet song we heard last night. Cesario, will you sing it?"

"I'm sorry, my lord," answered Cesario, "but I cannot sing that song. It was Feste you heard last night. He is not here today."

"Ah, that is a disappointment," said the Duke. Then he called his servant Curio. "Curio, go and find Feste," he said.

"Yes, my lord," said Curio. He left to go look for the clown.

The Duke turned back to the boy again. "Cesario, this love I feel causes me great pain," he said with disappointment. "Why won't Olivia return my love?" Then he asked Cesario, "How do you like the tune my musicians are playing now?"

"It truly echoes what the heart feels," said Cesario.

"Are you in love?" asked the Duke.

"A little, my lord."

"What kind of woman is she?"

"Like you, my lord. Her skin is the same color as yours."

"And how old?" asked Orsino.

"About your age, my lord," replied Cesario.

Just then Curio arrived with Feste. "Give us the song I heard you sing last night," commanded Orsino.

So Feste sang about a young man who loved a fair young woman. But the woman did not return the man's love, and he died.

"COME AWAY, COME AWAY, DEATH; FLY AWAY, FLY AWAY, BREATH," sang Feste.

Though the words were sad, the tune made Orsino feel better. The Duke handed Feste some gold coins. Then he asked everyone but Cesario to leave the room.

"Cesario, commanded the Duke, "go again to Olivia's. Tell that cruel woman who causes me pain that I love her."

"But she will not accept your love," answered Cesario.

"You must convince her!" said the Duke.

"What if there was some lady that loved you as much as you love Olivia. You cannot love her—and you tell her so. Must she then accept your answer?"

"My love is greater than anyone's," replied the Duke.

"My father," said Cesario, "had a daughter that loved a man. Perhaps it was in the same way that I might love you, my lord. That is, if I were a woman."

"What is her story?" asked Orsino.

"She never told him of her love," said Cesario. Viola wished she could tell the Duke that she was a woman, and that she loved him.

Viola could see that the Duke was very sad. "I shall go now to see your lady."

"Good," said Orsino. "And give her this jewel." He handed Cesario a beautiful gift for Olivia.

* * *

Sir Andrew and Sir Toby were in Olivia's garden.

"Won't you be glad to see that rascal Malvolio made a fool?" said Toby.

Maria came running over. She had a letter in her hand. It had Olivia's seal on it. "Crouch down behind the hedge and hide," said Maria. "Malvolio is coming. I'll drop the letter on the path."

Andrew and Toby crouched behind a green hedge. Maria dropped her letter on the path, then ran off to hide behind a tree.

Malvolio walked along the path talking to himself. Andrew and Toby peeked out from where they were hiding.

"Olivia treats me so well. I believe she could love me," he said to himself. Just then, he saw the letter at his feet. He stooped down to pick it up. "What's this? Why, it looks like my lady's seal! And the writing is my lady's. I wonder who this letter is for?"

"What's coming next will convince him," whispered Toby.

"Shhh," said Andrew.

I SEND THIS LETTER TO THE ONE I LOVE, read Malvolio. I COMMAND THE ONE I LOVE.

Malvolio thought about the words. Then, thinking out loud, "Why, she commands *me!* I serve her. This letter must be for me!" He read the rest of the letter. WEAR YELLOW STOCKINGS, AND ALWAYS SMILE WHEN YOU'RE AROUND ME.

Malvolio smiled. "It is *me* she loves!" Then he ran off happily.

When he was gone, Toby and Andrew came out from behind the hedge. Maria went over to them. "Watch what happens when that rascal starts wearing yellow stockings. Olivia *hates* that color! And he'll smile, which is wrong, because my lady's still mourning over her brother's death. If you want to see what happens next, come with me!"

Secrets and Tricks

COMPREHENSION CHECK

Choose the best answer.

1. The Duke's love for Olivia
____a. was causing him great pain.
____b. was making Cesario sick.
____c. was a disappointment to Curio.
____d. filled his soul with happiness.

2. The song Duke Orsino asked Feste to sing was
____a. a happy tune.
____b. a noisy tune.
____c. a sad love song.
____d. an old song.

3. When the Duke asked Cesario if he was in love,
____a. Viola chose her words carefully.
____b. Viola became uneasy.
____c. Viola suspected that Orsino was on to her disguise.
____d. Viola's stomach became upset.

4. Viola wished she could tell the Duke
____a. to quit wasting his time on Olivia.
____b. to stop wasting his money on Feste.
____c. to stop listening to music that makes him sad.
____d. that she was a woman - and in love with him.

5. The Duke
____a. is growing tired of Olivia.
____b. thinks that maybe he can buy Olivia's love.
____c. knows he will succeed in winning Olivia.
____d. knows that Cesario will never persuade Olivia to accept his love.

6. When did Maria drop her letter on the path?
____a. When she heard Malvolio talking to himself
____b. *Before* Malvolio walked in the garden
____c. After Andrew and Toby hid behind a hedge
____d. After she hid behind a tree

7. What made Malvolio think that the letter he found was written by Olivia?
____a. It had Olivia's seal on it.
____b. The writing looked like Olivia's.
____c. It smelled of his lady's perfume.
____d. a, and b

8. After reading the letter, Malvolio
____a. ran off happily.
____b. whistled a happy tune.
____c. bought some yellow stockings.
____d. went to see Olivia.

9. Another name for this story could be
____a. "The Letter."
____b. "Feste's Song."
____c. "A Gift for Olivia."
____d. "Having Fun."

10. This story is mainly about
____a. a love song.
____b. Duke Orsino's pain and Malvolio's joy.
____c. a cruel woman named Olivia.
____d. Olivia's lovely garden.

Check your answers with the Key on page 67.

This page may be reproduced for classroom use.

Secrets and Tricks

VOCABULARY CHECK

accept	command	crouch	disappointment	seal	stocking

I. Sentences to Finish
Fill in the blank in each sentence with the correct key word from the box above.

1. I couldn't hide my _____ in failing the road test.

2. The _____ on the letter showed it came from the President.

3. The dog jumped on Betty and put a run in her _____.

4. Will Joe _____ the job offer if it means moving to Dallas?

5. The captain gave the _____ to set sail at once.

6. I watched the cat _____ behind the barn waiting to catch the mouse.

II. Making Sense of Sentences
Put a check next to YES if the sentence makes sense. Put a check next to NO if the sentence does not make sense.

1. Mike showed great **disappointment** in winning the game.   ___YES ___NO

2. Billy had to **crouch** to get his kite out of the tree.   ___YES ___NO

3. Today I wore one black **stocking** and one blue **stocking** to work.   ___YES ___NO

4. The king put his **seal** on all important papers.   ___YES ___NO

5. I like all my teachers **accept** one.   ___YES ___NO

6. It was nice of you to **command** my dog while I was away.   ___YES ___NO

Check your answers with the Key on page 70.

This page may be reproduced for classroom use.

Pretending Brings Trouble

PREPARATION

Key Words

admire	(ad mīr´)	think highly of; respect *"I admire Harry for telling the truth,"* *said Ann.*
although	(ôl ŦHō´)	even though *Steven wanted to go swimming although* *it was raining.*
bet	(bet)	to be very sure; was very sure *Susan told Mary that she bet the teacher* *would give them a test on Friday.*
coax	(kōks)	use gentle ways to cause someone to do something *The young mother tried to coax her son* *into going to bed.*
dull	(dul)	not interesting *Mr. Thornton is a very dull person. He* *doesn't talk much.*
God	(god)	an all-powerful being who many believe is the maker and ruler of the world *When Jane got lost in the forest, she asked* *God to help her find her way home.*

Pretending Brings Trouble

Necessary Words

behalf   (bi haf´)   in the interest of
(on behalf of)

When Charlie's family moved to a new home, the neighbors brought over a cake. Charlie thanked them on behalf of his whole family.

excellent   (ek´ sl ənt)   very good; better than others

Miss Bates was an excellent teacher.
"This cake is excellent! Who made it?"

madam   (mad´ əm)   a polite title used when speaking of a lady or to a lady

"May I help you, madam?" asked the man in the shop.

niece   (nēs)   a daughter of one's brother or sister, or one's brother-in-law or sister-in-law

Because his sister wasn't feeling well, Sarah took her niece home for a few days.

pity   (pit´ ē)

1. to feel sorry for another's suffering or sorrow
 Jane felt pity for Alice when Alice broke her leg.
2. something to be sorry for
 It's a pity to stay in the house when the weather is so nice.

recently   (rē´snt lē)   not long ago

Recently, my father bought me a new puppy.

Pretending Brings Trouble

Cesario finds Feste in Olivia's garden.

Preview:
1. Read the name of the story.
2. Look at the picture.
3. Read the sentence under the picture.
4. Read the first seven paragraphs of the story.
5. Then answer the following question.

You learned from your preview that Feste lives near
____a. Olivia's house.
____b. Cesario's house.
____c. the church.
____d. the school.

Turn to the Comprehension Check on page 34 for the right answer.

Now read the story.
Read to find out why Sir Andrew wants to go home.

Pretending Brings Trouble

Viola (as Cesario) entered Olivia's garden. There he saw Feste holding a drum.

"Hello my friend," said Cesario. "Do you live by your drum?" He wanted to know if Feste earned his living by playing the drum.

"No, sir," replied Feste. "I live by the church."

"Are you a churchman?"

"Oh, no," Feste laughed. "I say I live by the church because I live in my house, and my house is near the church."

"Aren't you Lady Olivia's fool?" asked Cesario.

"She won't keep a real fool until she is married," replied Feste with a smile.

"I saw you recently at Duke Orsino's court. God bless you, sir." Cesario gave Feste some coins as a gift for his joking.

"Thank you sir, and may God give you a beard!" Feste was making fun of Cesario because his face was smooth like a woman's.

Just then Sir Toby and Sir Andrew appeared. "Good-day to you sir," said Toby to Cesario. "My niece would like you to come into the house and speak with her, if that is why you have come here today."

"But of course," said Cesario. "I am here to see your niece on behalf of Duke Orsino."

Then Olivia came outside.

"My most excellent Lady!" said Cesario.

"Leave us," commanded Olivia to the others. Only Olivia and Cesario remained in the garden.

"I am your faithful servant, my lady. I have come on behalf of my master, Duke Orsino." Although Cesario showed her the jewel from the Duke, Olivia did not take it.

"*My* servant, sir? You are the Duke's servant."

"And as he is your servant, then so am I. Madam, I come to ask you to think kindly of him."

"Oh, please stop!" said Olivia, angrily. "I ordered you not to speak of him again. But if *you* will begin courting *me*, I would gladly listen to your wooing."

"Dear lady. . ." began Cesario.

But Olivia put up her hand and said, "Please let me speak. After your last visit here, I sent you a ring. I should not have done that, but I could not help myself. It seems that you are not the man for me, for you are still very young. But, when you are fully grown, your wife will have a fine husband."

"Dear lady, I pity you, for I am not what you think I am." *Little does she know that I am not a man!* thought Viola. "Do you have a word to send to the Duke?"

"No, but how I wish you were what I want you to be!" *I wish he could by my husband*, thought Olivia. "Cesario, I love and admire you so much that I cannot hide my feelings no matter how I try!"

"Madam, no woman owns my heart and none ever shall," replied Cesario. "Farewell. I will not bother you again."

"Please come again," said Olivia. She could not bear to lose Cesario. *I will coax him into coming back*, she thought. Although she knew she could never love the Duke, she pretended that there was still a chance. That way, Cesario would have to return. "Perhaps you may still be able to make my heart accept Duke Orsino's love," she said.

*   *   *

Meanwhile, Sir Andrew and Sir Toby were talking. "I am going home," said Andrew in a trembling voice. "I won't stay a moment longer!"

"But why, my friend?" replied Toby. He wanted Andrew to stay.

"I saw Olivia with Orsino's servant. She must admire him. She's never that nice to me! She thinks I am dull."

"So that is what is troubling you," said Toby. *It would be a pity if he left now*, thought Toby. *I must coax him into staying.* "Never fear, my friend. Most times when a woman treats you poorly, it just means that she is in love with you."

Andrew became angry. He looked at his friend. "Are you trying to make a fool of me?"

"Of course not!" replied Toby. "I bet my niece was just trying to make you jealous. You should have shown your jealousy. You missed your chance. But there may still be a way."

Andrew's face seemed to brighten. "*Jealous*, you say? Tell me what you think I should do," he said eagerly, believing everything that Toby said.

"You must challenge Cesario to a duel!"

After giving it some thought, Andrew replied, "That's an excellent idea."

Well, go write it then," said Toby. "I will bring him your letter when it's finished."

Andrew ran off, thinking about what to write. Toby sat down and rubbed his hands together. *It has been fun to have Sir Andrew here*, thought Toby. *But recently, things have grown dull. I need more excitement, and I bet this will do the trick!*

Pretending Brings Trouble

COMPREHENSION CHECK

Choose the best answer.

> **Preview Answer:**
> c. the church.

1. Feste earned his living
   ____a. playing the drum.
   ____b. taking care of Olivia's garden.
   ____c. singing.
   ____d. amusing Olivia and her guests.

2. Cesario gave Feste some coins
   ____a. as a gift for his joking.
   ____b. to buy some new plants for Olivia's garden.
   ____c. to give to the church.
   ____d. to buy a new drum.

3. Feste made fun of Cesario's
   ____a. music.
   ____b. beard.
   ____c. smooth face.
   ____d. soft hands.

4. First Cesario met Feste in the garden. Then Sir Toby and Sir Andrew appeared. Who entered the garden next?
   ____a. Duke Orsino
   ____b. Olivia
   ____c. Malvolio
   ____d. Viola

5. Olivia wouldn't accept the jewel from the Duke because
   ____a. it was very small.
   ____b. it wasn't worth any money.
   ____c. she didn't want to feel like she owed the Duke anything.
   ____d. she had so much jewelry already.

6. Olivia tells Cesario
   ____a. to stop coming around.
   ____b. that he is too young to be working for the Duke.
   ____c. that he is a man of few words.
   ____d. that she loves and admires him.

7. Olivia tried to coax Cesario into returning again by telling him that
   ____a. she wanted him to be more than her friend.
   ____b. on his next visit she would cook his favorite meal.
   ____c. there was still a chance that she could love Orsino.
   ____d. she would keep the Duke's jewel if he promised to come back.

8. Toby coaxed Andrew into staying a while longer by making him believe
   ____a. he still had a chance with Olivia.
   ____b. Olivia had always loved him.
   ____c. he could make Olivia jealous.
   ____d. he brought a lot of excitement to Olivia's home.

9. Another name for this story could be
   ____a. "Viola's Disguise Brings Many Surprises."
   ____b. "The Faithful Servant."
   ____c. "Challenged to a Duel."
   ____d. "Olivia's Lovely Garden."

10. This story is mainly about
    ____a. how Toby tricks Andrew into staying.
    ____b. Olivia's feelings for Cesario.
    ____c. how Viola's lie keeps getting bigger and bigger.
    ____d. how Feste earned his money.

Check your answers with the Key on page 67.

This page may be reproduced for classroom use.

Pretending Brings Trouble

VOCABULARY CHECK

admire	although	bet	coax	dull	God

I. Sentences to Finish
Fill in the blank in each sentence with the correct key word from the box above.

1. People often pray to _____ in times of trouble.

2. I _____ Rita for taking such good care of her father during his long illness.

3. I studied hard before taking the test. I _____ I passed with flying colors!

4. Using a banana, the zookeeper tried to _____ the monkey back into its cage.

5. _____ I don't eat red meat, when I'm invited for dinner, I eat it to be polite.

6. I wasn't at all interested in reading that _____ book!

II. Word Search
All the words above are hidden in the puzzle below. They may be written from left to right, up and down, or on an angle. As you find each word, put a circle around it. One word, that is not a key word, has been done for you.

```
A D M I R E X E
C U O G O B C L
O L D U L E O T
A L T H O U G H
X U X A D M O O
S I T B E T D S
```

Check your answers with the Key on page 70.

This page may be reproduced for classroom use.

Malvolio is Made the Fool

PREPARATION

Key Words

arrest   (ə rest´)   to seize and take to jail or court
> *I saw the policeman <u>arrest</u> the man for stealing.*

explore   (eks plôr´)   1. to travel over little-known lands, seas, or outer space to discover new things
> *Jack's family took a trip to <u>explore</u> the island of Hawaii.*

    2. examine carefully
> *The boys wanted to <u>explore</u> the cave.*

grateful   (grāt´ fəl)   thankful
> *"I would be <u>grateful</u> if you would help me carry these bags," said Mrs. Smith to her son Tommy.*

hadn't   (had´ nt)   had not
> *John <u>hadn't</u> been on an airplane before, so he was a little scared.*

port   (pôrt)   a place where ships and boats park to load and unload goods; harbor
> *Our boat pulled into <u>port</u> at six o'clock in the morning.*

property   (prop´ ər tē)   a thing or things owned
> *That big house on the hill is Mr. Smith's <u>property</u>.*

Malvolio is Made the Fool

Necessary Words

devil (dev´ l) an evil spirit some call Satan
Some people believe that the <u>devil</u> can make them do strange things.

entertain (en´ tər tān´) to keep pleasantly interested; to please or amuse
When Jane came over after school, Mary showed a film to <u>entertain</u> her.

nervous (nėr´ vəs) easily excited or upset; not able to rest
Fran is <u>nervous</u> about being left alone at night.

prayers (prãrz) special words spoken to God
"I will keep you in my <u>prayers</u>."
"Have you said your <u>prayers</u> yet?" asked Mother.

sensible (sen´ sə bl) having or showing good sense or judgement; wise
Karen is too <u>sensible</u> to fall for your silly joke.

Malvolio is Made the Fool

Sebastian tells Antonio, "I want to explore this new country."

> **Preview:**   1. Read the name of the story.
> 2. Look at the picture.
> 3. Read the sentence under the picture.
> 4. Read the first six paragraphs of the story.
> 5. Then answer the following question.
>
> You learned from your preview that Antonio
> ____a. had followed Sebastian to town.
> ____b. had left Sebastian on the shore.
> ____c. wanted to go exploring with Sebastian.
> ____d. had never been to Illyria.
>
> *Turn to the Comprehension Check on page 40 for the right answer.*

Now read the story.
Read to find out why Olivia asks Toby to watch over Malvolio.

Malvolio is Made the Fool

"I could not stay away from you, my friend," said Antonio to Sebastian.

They were in the main town of Illyria. Sebastian had left Antonio on the shore. He hadn't expected to see him again. But Antonio had followed him to town.

"I was worried about you. You have never been to Illyria before."

"Kind Antonio, I am grateful," said Sebastian. "Let's take a look around."

"First we had better find a place to stay," replied Antionio.

"But I'm not tired," answered Sebastian, excitedly. "I want to explore this new country."

"I'm sorry, but as I told you before, I'm in danger here. Once I was in a sea fight with one of Orsino's ships. It was on its way to another country's port to sell some things. I'm afraid the Duke might send someone to arrest me if he discovers I am here," said Antonio, in a nervous voice.

Sebastian looked puzzled. "I don't understand. Had you killed one of his seamen?"

"No, I hadn't. But I took some of Orsino's property. I took the property for myself and sold it at port."

"You must be careful then. You must not walk around so openly," said Sebastian. "I don't want to see you get arrested."

"Yes, but I don't like to hide either. Here, take these," said Antonio. He handed Sebastian some gold coins. "Enjoy your time here and explore the town. I will go to the inn called *Elephant* and wait for you there."

And so Antonio and Sebastian parted ways a second time.

*   *   *

Olivia and Maria were in the garden. Olivia waited for Cesario. She had asked him to come visit again. "I am so nervous, Maria. How shall I entertain him?"

Maria didn't give an answer. Her lady was just talking out loud to herself.

Olivia walked up and down the same spot. "Where is my servant Malvolio?" she cried. "Why, he is sensible. Perhaps he has an idea about how I can entertain my company."

Just then, Maria saw Malvolio walking toward them. "Here he comes, madam," said Maria. "But I must warn you. He's been acting strange lately. All he does is smile. I think there's something wrong with him."

Malvolio entered the garden with a big smile on his face.

"How are you, Malvolio?" asked Olivia.

"Very well, thank you!" he replied in a loud, happy voice. Then he smiled widely and winked his eye.

"Stop smiling!" snapped Olivia. "I want to talk with you. I am nervous about something. I know you're a sensible man. Perhaps you can help me."

"There is nothing to be nervous about," said Malvolio, as if he knew what bothered her.

Olivia didn't know what to make of the strange way he was acting. "What is the matter with you today?" she asked. "And why are you smiling when you know I'm troubled?"

"I smile because I found your letter. I recognized your writing. And you can be sure I will carry out your orders," said Malvolio proudly. Then he winked again.

"I think you need some rest," said Olivia. "Maybe I work you too hard."

Malvolio answered by kissing his hand and blowing the kisses in Olivia's direction.

"Heaven help you!" shouted Olivia. "Why do you smile like that and kiss your hand?"

"I remembered the yellow stockings," answered Malvolio sweetly. He pointed to his legs. He hadn't any idea that it was Maria who had written the letter!

"Why, you are mad!" exclaimed Olivia. She turned to Maria. "Maria, go get Toby. Tell him I would be grateful if he would watch over Malvolio. Have Toby put him away where he will come to no harm."

Just then a servant entered the garden. "My lady," he said, "your company has arrived."

"Thank you," said Olivia, nervously. She still had no idea how she would entertain Cesario.

Maria followed Olivia into the house. A few minutes later, Maria came out with Sir Toby. They went into the garden.

"Why don't you come with me," Toby said to Malvolio, taking him by the arm.

"Go away!" shouted Malvolio, pulling away. "I want nothing to do with you!"

"I think the devil has taken hold of him," said Maria.

"Oh, that's very funny---the devil ha! ha!" laughed Malvolio.

Toby took hold of Malvolio's arm again. But once more, Malvolio pulled away. "Let me be!" he shouted.

"He needs our prayers," said Maria.

"I'll say my own prayers!" he shouted, marching back to the house.

"He's fallen for our trick!" said Sir Toby, laughing. "Come on, Maria, we will put him in a dark room."

Malvolio is Made the fool

COMPREHENSION CHECK

Choose the best answer.

> **Preview Answer:**
> a. had followed Sebastian to town.

1. If Antonio was found in Illyria, _____ would have him arrested.
   - ____a. Olivia
   - ____b. Malvolio
   - ____c. Duke Orsino
   - ____d. Sir Toby

2. Antonio would be arrested for
   - ____a. killing one of the Duke's men.
   - ____b. sinking one of the Duke's ships.
   - ____c. selling goods at port.
   - ____d. stealing.

3. Sebastian was _____ to explore Illyria.
   - ____a. eager
   - ____b. afraid
   - ____c. grateful
   - ____d. amazed

4. While Sebastian went exploring, Antonio waited for him at a place called
   - ____a. The Elephant Inn.
   - ____b. The Eagle's Nest.
   - ____c. The River's Edge.
   - ____d. The Great Escape.

5. Olivia had always thought Malvolio to be
   - ____a. a nervous fellow.
   - ____b. a sensible man.
   - ____c. a silly fool.
   - ____d. a devil.

6. The strange way Malvolio acted caused Olivia to believe he might be
   - ____a. troubled.
   - ____b. nervous about something.
   - ____c. losing his mind.
   - ____d. up to no good.

7. Olivia called Malvolio "mad" and sent for Sir Toby *right after*
   - ____a. Malvolio blew kisses in her direction.
   - ____b. he pointed to the yellow stockings he wore.
   - ____c. he told Olivia he had found her letter.
   - ____d. Cesario arrived.

8. Malvolio became angry because
   - ____a. Maria said the devil had a hold on him.
   - ____b. Maria said she would pray for him.
   - ____c. Sir Toby put his hands on him.
   - ____d. he realized he had been tricked.

9. Another name for this story could be
   - ____a. "Praying for the Devil."
   - ____b. "Entertaining Company."
   - ____c. "Malvolio Takes the Bait."
   - ____d. "Blowing Kisses."

10. This story is mainly about
    - ____a. how Malvolio had fallen for Maria's clever trick.
    - ____b. why Antonio had followed Sebastian.
    - ____c. why the Duke had it in for Antonio.
    - ____d. why Olivia was nervous about seeing Cesario again.

Check your answers with the Key on page 67.

This page may be reproduced for classroom use.

Malvolio is Made the Fool

VOCABULARY CHECK

arrest	explore	grateful	hadn't	port	property

I. Sentences to Finish
Fill in the blank in each sentence with the correct key word from the box above.

1. "I'm very _____ for those tickets you gave me to the big game."

2. If I _____ looked before crossing the street, that car would have hit me.

3. That shiny new car is the _____ of Jerry Randall.

4. The ship pulled into _____ to unload its goods.

5. The officer placed the thief under _____.

6. Little boys like to _____ new places.

II. Put an X next to the best ending for each sentence.

1. Sam was ***grateful***
   ____a. for the ride.
   ____b. that he lost his hat.

2. We went to the ***port***
   ____a. to meet Jim's ship.
   ____b. to catch the train.

3. Let's go ***explore***
   ____a. the journey.
   ____b. the island.

4. Phyllis ***hadn't***
   ____a. everything to wear.
   ____b. told the truth.

5. Dan's ***property***
   ____a. belongs to everyone.
   ____b. belongs to Dan.

6. If you ***arrest*** someone,
   ____a. he won't be a free man.
   ____b. he's a danger to himself.

Check your answers with the Key on page 70.

Drawing Swords

PREPARATION

Key Words

contain   (kən tān´)   1. hold back one's feelings
       Jill couldn't <u>contain</u> her excitement over winning the contest.
    2. to have within itself; hold as contents
       The book <u>contained</u> many stories about life.

dignity   (dig´ nə tē)   proud and self-respecting manner
    Laurie kept her <u>dignity</u>, even when people said unfair things about her.

habit   (hab´ it)   practice; custom
    Bradley has a bad <u>habit</u> of biting his nails.

lad   (lad)   boy
    The <u>lad</u> has grown taller since I last saw him.

thankful   (thangk´ fəl)   feeling or showing thanks; grateful
    Russell was <u>thankful</u> for all Jim's help.

treat   (trēt)   care for; act toward
    The man does not <u>treat</u> his horses well.

Drawing Swords

Necessary Words

enemy   (en´ ə mē)   person or group that hates and tries to harm another
enemies   (en´ ə mēz)
> *After their fight, Jim said to Bob, "I want to be your friend, not your <u>enemy</u>."*
> *Charles has many friends and few <u>enemies</u>.*

escort   (es´ kôrt)   one or more persons going with other persons to see that they keep safe, or to honor them
> *The President always has an <u>escort</u> with him.*

offend   (ə fend´)   to hurt the feelings of someone; make angry
> *Jack was angry with Steve, but Steve didn't understand what he had done to <u>offend</u> Jack.*

officer   (ôf´ ə sər)   someone who holds a public or government office, such as a police officer
> *When the <u>officer</u> saw the man stealing the woman's bag, he began to chase him.*

sword   (sôrd)   a weapon with a long, sharp blade fastened to a handle
> *Jim's father owns a <u>sword</u> that is more than three hundred years old.*

Drawing Swords

"Here," said Olivia, as she handed Cesario a necklace.

Preview:
1. Read the name of the story.
2. Look at the picture.
3. Read the sentence under the picture.
4. Read the first six paragraphs of the story.
5. Then answer the following question.

You learned from your preview that Olivia's necklace contains
_____a. Olivia's picture.
_____b. a picture of Olivia's mother.
_____c. a picture of Duke Orsino.
_____d. a letter.

Turn to the Comprehension Check on page 46 for the right answer.

Now read the story.
Read to find out what happens as Sir Andrew and Cesario draw swords.

Drawing Swords

Olivia spoke to Cesario (Viola). "I have spoken again about my feelings for you. I am sorry," she said, "but, it is hard for me to contain myself."

"In the same way," replied Cesario, "my master finds it hard not to tell you of his love for you."

"Here," said Olivia, as she handed him a necklace. "Wear this chain with a case that contains my picture. If you ask anything of me, I will give it to you."

"Only this," said Cesario, "that you would give your love to my master."

"How can I give that to *him* when I have already given it to *you*?" Olivia smiled sweetly and asked him to come again tomorrow.

Cesario bowed and left.

* * *

Sir Toby and Maria were in the garden. Sir Andrew came over to them and handed Toby a letter. "Here's the challenge I wrote to Cesario!" said Andrew. He wanted Olivia to treat him the way she treated Cesario.

"'YOU COME TO SEE LADY OLIVIA,'" read Toby, "'AND RIGHT IN FRONT OF ME SHE TREATS YOU WELL. BUT, YOU ARE LYING ABOUT SOMETHING. I JUST KNOW IT.'"

"Very good," said Toby after he read the letter. "I will take your letter to that rascal Cesario."

"I will wait at the other end of the garden!" said Andrew. Then he ran off.

"This is poorly written," said Toby to Maria, when they were alone again. "I'll tell Cesario about the challenge in my own words."

Maria saw Cesario walking toward them. "Here he comes," said Maria. Then she went into the house.

"God save you, sir," said Toby to Cesario. "Draw your sword, for your enemy waits for you at the end of the garden!"

"There must be some mistake!" said Cesario. "I have no enemies. Please, sir, tell me who he is."

"He is a man of honor, but a devil when he's fighting. He once killed several men," said Toby, trying to frighten him.

Viola, very frightened, said, "Then I must return to the house and ask the lady for an escort!"

"No, sir, you shall not go back to the house for an escort - unless you want to fight me!" shouted Toby.

"Please, sir, I would be thankful to know what I did to offend him," begged Cesario.

"*Fabian!*" called Toby to one of Olivia's servants. Fabian came running out of the house. "Watch this man and do not let him escape!" Then Toby went to talk to Andrew.

Viola became more nervous. She did not know that all this was just one of Toby's tricks. Fabian knew about the trick, but he played along.

"Please help me, sir. It is not my habit to fight!" exclaimed Cesario.

"Perhaps we can talk with the man who has challenged you," said Fabian.

"I would be very thankful," said Cesario.

Meanwhile, Toby was talking to Andrew and scaring *him*. "That lad Cesario is a devil! He is sharp with a sword, with a sharper temper still."

Now Sir Andrew became nervous. "If I had known he was so good with a sword, I never would have challenged him. Please, friend, talk to him for me. Tell him I'll give him my horse if he will not fight me."

Toby went back to Fabian and whispered, "Andrew is ready to give up his horse so he won't have to fight."

Fabian replied in a whisper, "This lad is just as afraid of Andrew."

Toby turned to Cesario and said, "Andrew doesn't really want to fight you, but he must keep his dignity. Draw your sword. He won't hurt you."

God help me, thought Viola. *In another minute I may have to tell them that I'm not really a man!*

Then Toby returned to Andrew and said, "Draw your sword, my friend. This man must save his dignity. But he promised he wouldn't hurt you."

When Andrew and Cesario stood before each other, they both drew their swords. At that very moment a man rushed toward them. It was Antonio. He thought Cesario was Sebastian, Viola's twin. He thought Sebastian was in trouble. "*Stop!*" he shouted. "If this young gentleman has offended you, I will duel with you on his behalf!"

A police officer suddenly appeared. Looking at Antonio he said, "I arrest you on the order of Count Orsino!"

"You mistake me for somebody else," said Antonio nervously.

"I'm not in the habit of forgetting a face," replied the officer. "I know very well who you are, and you're not aboard your ship *now*."

Antonio looked at Cesario. "I'm sorry, my friend, I must go. But, please give me back my money, for I need it now."

Viola, not knowing what he was talking about, said, "I have never seen you before."

"Sebastian, how could you forget the kindness I have shown you?" said Antonio, as the officer led him away.

He called me Sebastian! thought Viola. *Could it be that my brother lives, and that this man thinks I am he? Oh, please let it be true!*

𝔇rawing 𝔖wor𝔡s

COMPREHENSION CHECK

Choose the best answer.

1. Olivia gave Cesario a _____ to wear.
   ____a. shirt
   ____b. hat
   ____c. necklace
   ____d. ring

2. What did Sir Toby say about the letter Sir Andrew had written to Cesario?
   ____a. It was much too long.
   ____b. It was written by a rascal.
   ____c. It was written by a poor man.
   ____d. It was poorly written.

3. Toby decided to tell Cesario about Andrew's challenge in
   ____a. his own words.
   ____b. the morning.
   ____c. the evening.
   ____d. after lunch.

4. Toby tricked Sir Andrew and Cesario by
   ____a. hiding their swords.
   ____b. making each think that the other was stronger and more fierce.
   ____c. telling each of them that they were not good fighters.
   ____d. saying he would give each of them a horse if they didn't fight.

5. Toby told Andrew that Cesario
   ____a. had an old sword that couldn't harm a fly.
   ____b. had more important things to do than fight.
   ____c. was sharp with a sword and had a bad temper.
   ____d. was afraid of him.

6. Toby told Cesario that Andrew
   ____a. didn't know how to fight.
   ____b. had once had a fight with the devil.
   ____c. had once killed several men.
   ____d. was not a man of honor.

7. First Andrew and Cesario drew their swords. Then, Antonio rushed toward them. Next,
   ____a. an officer of the law arrested Antonio.
   ____b. a police officer sent Antonio back to his ship.
   ____c. a police officer stopped the duel.
   ____d. Cesario returned Antonio's money.

8. Antonio thought Cesario was Sebastian because
   ____a. Cesario's voice sounded like Sebastian's.
   ____b. Cesario looked exactly like Sebastian.
   ____c. Cesario was wearing Sebastian's clothes.
   ____d. Cesario and Sebastian had the same color eyes.

9. Another name for this story could be
   ____a. "Cesario Begs for an Escort."
   ____b. "A Gift for Cesario."
   ____c. "Antonio Stops a Duel."
   ____d. "A Man of Honor."

10. This story is mainly about
    ____a. Olivia's feelings for Cesario.
    ____b. men of honor.
    ____c. Antonio's arrest.
    ____d. how Sir Toby tries to stop the challenge by duel made by Sir Andrew.

Check your answers with the Key on page 67.

This page may be reproduced for classroom use.

Drawing Swords

VOCABULARY CHECK

contain	dignity	habit	lad	thankful	treat

I. Sentences to Finish
Fill in the blank in each sentence with the correct key word from the box above.

1. I was taught to always _____older people with respect.

2. Though Mother grew up in a poor home, she always kept her _____.

3. John was _____ that his sister always helped him with his homework.

4. How many jellybeans does that jar _____?

5. Greg has a bad _____of talking with food in his mouth.

6. "Will the young _____in the yellow shirt please take a seat," said Mrs. Roth.

II. Hidden Word
In the spaces, write the key word that fits each definition. Unscramble the circled letters to find the name of a character in the story.

1. to have within itself; hold as contents
   1. __ __ ◯ __ __ __ __

2. feeling or showing thanks; grateful
   2. __ __ __ __ __ ◯ __ __

3. proud and self-respecting manner
   3. __ __ __ ◯ __ __ __

4. practice; custom
   4. __ __ ◯ __ __ __

5. boy
   5. __ ◯ __

6. care for; act toward
   6. __ __ __ ◯ __

The name of the character is _____.

Check your answers with the Key on page 71.

This page may be reproduced for classroom use.

The Struggle

PREPARATION

Key Words

ache (āk) a pain or hurt that goes on and on
Jackie felt an <u>ache</u> in her heart when she saw the sick puppy.

mystery (mis´ tər ē) something that is hidden or unknown; secret
It was a <u>mystery</u> to everyone how the cat got into the clothes dryer.

nuisance (nü´ sns) something or someone that annoys, troubles, or offends
Flies are a <u>nuisance</u>.

quit (kwit) stop
"<u>Quit</u> taking my things," said Sally to her little sister.

remove (ri müv´) take away
Dr. O'Neal will <u>remove</u> Jack's tooth today.

shoulder (shōl´ dər) a part of the body to which the arm is attached
The ache in Mr. Brown's <u>shoulder</u> is such a nuisance to him.

The Struggle

Necessary Words

agree   (ə grē′)   to have the same feeling; to believe something in the same way as someone else does
Karen and Sue are good friends. They <u>agree</u> on just about everything.

dagger   (dag′ ər)   a small weapon with a short, pointed blade
The thief hid his <u>dagger</u> under his shirt.

realize   (rē′ ə līz)   clearly understand
"I <u>realize</u> how hard you worked to save all that money," said Dad.

The Struggle

"Find Cesario for me, Feste," says Olivia, "and bring him here. Tell him it's important."

Preview: 1. Read the name of the story.
2. Look at the picture.
3. Read the sentences under the picture.
4. Read the first ten paragraphs of the story.
5. Then answer the following question.

You learned from your preview that
_____a. Sir Toby wants to beat Cesario.
_____b. Sir Andrew wants to beat Cesario.
_____c. Sir Andrew is a cowardly rabbit.
_____d. Fabian is a cowardly rabbit.

Turn to the Comprehension Check on page 52 for the right answer.

Now read the story.
Read to find out who Feste brings back to Olivia's house.

The Struggle

Cesario had just left to go back to the Duke's court. Sir Toby, Sir Andrew and Fabian were in Olivia's garden talking about him.

"He's a coward if I ever saw one!" said Fabian.

"I agree," said Toby. "He is more cowardly than a rabbit!"

"I'll find him and beat him!" shouted Andrew, waving his sword about.

Toby became nervous. "Yes, beat him, but don't draw your swor. . ."

But, Andrew ran off before Toby had finished speaking.

"Come," said Fabian. "Let's see what happens."

"I'll bet it will come to nothing," said Toby, as the two of them went off to follow Andrew.

Just then Olivia came out of the house with Feste, the clown.

"Find Cesario for me, Feste, and bring him here. Tell him it's important."

So Feste went to search for Cesario. Olivia walked slowly back inside the house thinking, *I want so much to see Cesario. I have this terrible ache in my heart. I asked him to return tomorrow, but that's too long for me to wait.*

Later, Feste returned to the garden with Sebastian. Feste was certain Sebastian was Cesario. (For Sebastian and his sister looked exactly alike. It was hard to tell one apart from the other.)

Feste looked at Sebastian. "So you're telling me that your name is not Cesario? Then my name is not Feste either!"

"Quit your joking," said Sebastian. "Let me be."

The way Feste was behaving was a mystery to Sebastian. He didn't realize that his sister was alive and pretending to be a man named Cesario.

"You're pretending that you don't know me," said Feste. "Then in that case, I don't know you either! You say your name is not Cesario?" Then he pointed to his own nose. "Then this is not *my* nose!"

"Go play your jokes on someone else," said Sebastian. He reached into his pocket for some gold coins to give Feste so that he would leave him alone. At just that moment, Sir Andrew appeared, carrying his sword.

"Ah, so we meet again!" said Andrew to Sebastian. (He thought Sebastian was Cesario.) "I have something for you!" And with those words, he hit Sebastian on the shoulder.

"And I have something for you, as well!" said Sebastian. Then he hit Andrew's shoulder with the handle of his dagger. "And this!" he said. Then he hit him again.

These people must be mad! thought Sebastian. *First the clown called me Cesario, and now another man has started a fight with me!*

Toby and Fabian came running over. Toby grabbed Sebastian's arm with both hands. "Quit hitting him, sir! Put away that dagger!"

"I'm going to tell my lady Olivia about this," said Feste, walking toward the house.

"I'll take him to a court of law for striking me," exclaimed Andrew. "Even though I struck him first, I don't care!"

"Remove your hands!" shouted Sebastian to Toby, struggling to get away.

"I will *not* remove them!"

shouted Toby, holding him tightly. "Put away your dagger!"

Suddenly Sebastian broke free and drew his sword. "What do you want of me? Draw your sword if you dare!"

So Toby drew his sword.

"*Stop!*" yelled Olivia, as she ran out from the house. "I order you to stop! Will you never realize what a nuisance you are? You should go and live in a cave where you don't need any manners." Turning now to Sebastian she said, "Dear Cesario, don't be offended." Then she turned back to Toby. "*Go!* Get out of my sight!"

So Toby and Andrew left in a hurry.

"My dear, sweet friend," said Olivia to Sebastian, "please be wise. Do not let your anger get the better of you. You don't know how many times my uncle has behaved badly. He plays stupid jokes on people. He's such a nuisance. But today he went too far. It made my heart ache to see him draw his sword against you."

What does all this mean? thought Sebastian. *This is all such a mystery. I don't understand what is happening. I have never seen this beautiful lady before today. But she acts as though she knows me - and loves me! If I am dreaming, let me sleep on, for this lady is a delight!*

"Please agree to come with me," said Olivia. "I want so much to marry you. Will you marry me?" she asked.

"I will," answered Sebastian.

The Struggle

COMPREHENSION CHECK

Choose the best answer.

1. Sir Andrew left Olivia's in a hurry to look for
   ____a. Cesario.
   ____b. Sebastian.
   ____c. trouble.
   ____d. something to eat.

2. Olivia sent Feste to find Cesario because
   ____a. she wanted to tell him that Andrew was after him.
   ____b. she wanted to give him a sword so he could fight Andrew.
   ____c. she couldn't wait until tomorrow to see him.
   ____d. she wouldn't be able to see him tomorrow.

3. Feste returned to Olivia's with
   ____a. Cesario.
   ____b. Sebastian.
   ____c. Sir Andrew.
   ____d. Sir Toby.

4. Feste thought Sebastian was Cesario because
   ____a. they both sounded alike.
   ____b. they both wore their hair the same way.
   ____c. they both wore the same clothes.
   ____d. the two looked exactly alike.

5. Sebastian thought Feste
   ____a. was playing a joke on him.
   ____b. was behaving like a coward.
   ____c. was looking for money.
   ____d. was a funny-looking clown.

6. Sebastian thought he could get rid of Feste
   ____a. by playing along with the joke.
   ____b. by paying him off.
   ____c. by acting very mysterious.
   ____d. by waving his sword about.

7. First, Andrew mistakes Sebastian for Cesario and hits him. Then, Sebastian hits him back with the handle of his dagger. Next,
   ____a. Toby grabbed Sebastian's arm with both hands.
   ____b. Sebastian drew his sword.
   ____c. Sebastian hit Andrew again.
   ____d. Olivia came running out of the house to stop the fight.

8. Sebastian didn't know what was happening to him. But he played along
   ____a. when Olivia called him a dear, sweet friend.
   ____b. when Olivia called Toby a nuisance.
   ____c. when Olivia stopped the fight.
   ____d. when Olivia asked him to marry her.

9. Another name for this story could be
   ____a. "Caught!"
   ____b. "Sebastian Meets Olivia."
   ____c. "Sebastian's Dream."
   ____d. "Feste's Joke."

10. This story is mainly about
   ____a. how Sebastian finds himself in trouble when he is mistaken for someone else.
   ____b. Feste's strange behavior.
   ____c. why Olivia called Toby a nuisance.
   ____d. Sebastian agreeing to marry Olivia.

Check your answers with the Key on page 67.

This page may be reproduced for classroom use.

The Struggle

VOCABULARY CHECK

ache	mystery	nuisance	quit	remove	shoulder

I. Sentences to Finish
Fill in the blank in each sentence with the correct key word from the box above.

1. How my dog, missing for six years, found his way home, remains a _____ to me.

2. Pete helped his father _____ the boxes from the garage.

3. Sara had a tummy _____ from eating so much candy.

4. Rabbits are a _____ in the vegetable garden.

5. Tara has _____-length hair.

6. "_____ bothering me," said Amy.

II. Put an X next to the best ending for each sentence.

1. It remains a *mystery* to me
   ____a. how money grows on trees.
   ____b. how the boat made it through the storm.
2. Russell had an *ache* in his knee
   ____a. that kept him out of the game.
   ____b. that made his father proud.
3. It is polite to *remove* your hat before
   ____a. brushing your teeth.
   ____b. sitting down at the table.

4. Jack hurt his *shoulder*
   ____a. carrying a box of feathers.
   ____b. playing football.
5. Sally is a *nuisance* because
   ____a. she's so kind.
   ____b. she never stops talking.
6. Sue promised to *quit*
   ____a. my job.
   ____b. smoking.

Check your answers with the Key on page 71.

This page may be reproduced for classroom use.

𝔥elp is on the 𝔚ay

PREPARATION

Key Words

breathe   (brēTH)   to draw air into the lungs (breathing organs) through the nose or mouth, and send it out again
> *Mary wanted to move to the country where she could <u>breathe</u> clean, fresh air.*

fortunate   (fôr´ chə nit)   lucky (having good things happen by chance)
> *Mike and Phyllis were <u>fortunate</u> to have had ten healthy children.*

imitate   (im´ ə tāt)   to try to be like, or act like, or sound like another
> *The boy likes to <u>imitate</u> his older brother.*

ink   (ingk)   a liquid used for writing, printing, or drawing
> *Not long ago, people had to dip their pens in a bottle of <u>ink</u> in order to write with them.*

nonsense   (non´ sens)   words, ideas, or acts without meaning; foolish talk or doings
> *That story Robert told is nothing but <u>nonsense</u>!*

robin   (rob´ ən)   a large bird with a red or orange breast
> *I saw a <u>robin</u> fly past my window.*

Help is on the Way

Necessary Words

fake   (fāk)   not real
> *Jane bought a <u>fake</u> fur coat to keep warm this winter.*

ignorance (ig´ nə rəns) without knowledge
> *Joe crashed his boat because of his <u>ignorance</u> of the rules of boating.*

minister (min´ ə stər) one who serves a church
> *The <u>minister</u> helped Frank forgive his father.*

peace   (pēs)
1. quiet and order; freedom from war or fighting
   > *Let there be <u>peace</u> on Earth.*
2. calmness of mind or of one's surroundings
   > *"I'd like some <u>peace</u> and quiet!" shouted Mother.*

priest   (prēst)   a special servant of God
> *The <u>priest</u> said a prayer for my grandmother who died today.*

Help is on the Way

Feste puts on a robe and fake beard.

Preview:
1. Read the name of the story.
2. Look at the picture.
3. Read the sentence under the picture.
4. Read the first four paragraphs of the story.
5. Then answer the following question.

You learned from your preview that Maria and Sir Toby

_____a. sent a letter to Malvolio.

_____b. were playing a trick on Feste.

_____c. were going to play another trick on Malvolio.

_____d. brought the minister to see Malvolio.

Turn to the Comprehension Check on page 58 for the right answer.

Now read the story.
Read to find out how Malvolio reacts to the trick!

Help is on the Way

"Put on this robe and fake beard," Maria told Feste. "If Malvolio should see you, he will think you are Sir Topas, the minister."

Malvolio had been locked in a dark room. He had found the letter Maria wrote. . .the one with Olivia's seal on it. He thought Olivia loved him. He had put on yellow stockings and smiled all the time. But, he was only doing what he believed Olivia wanted! But, Olivia had thought him mad and had him locked away. Maria and Toby had tricked him! Now, they wanted to play *another* trick.

Feste put on the robe and fake beard. He went to the room where Malvolio was kept. Maria and Toby followed and stood behind him.

Feste spoke through the keyhole. He changed his voice to sound like the minister's. "Peace be to you," he said.

"Who calls there?" came Malvolio's voice.

"It is Sir Topas," answered Feste.

Toby whispered to Maria. "He can really imitate Sir Topas."

Malvolio became excited. "Oh, Sir Topas! Please go to my lady. Tell her they have put me in this dark room!"

"Do you say the room is dark?" asked Feste, smiling.

"It's as dark as night, Sir."

"Madman, you are mistaken. There is no darkness but ignorance."

"But, Sir Topas, I am not *mad*! I tell you, this room is dark!"

Feste turned to Maria and Toby. Now all three were smiling. Speaking through the keyhole once again, Feste said, "Your room has windows. Yet, you say it's dark. That is nonsense, Madman. You are mistaken. Farewell, you must remain where you are."

"*Wait!*" called Malvolio.

Toby tapped Feste on the shoulder. "Speak to him in your own voice now," he said.

So Feste began to sing in his own voice. "Hey robin, jolly robin, tell me how your lady does."

"*Why, it's the Fool!*" exclaimed Malvolio, thinking that Feste had come along just as Sir Topas left. "Don't sing me your silly songs, Fool!" he shouted to Feste.

"My lady is unkind, indeed, to keep you in this room," said Feste.

"*Fool!*" repeated Malvolio.

"My lady loves another," sang Feste.

Malvolio was beginning to realize that he would get no help by speaking unkindly. "Good, Fool," he said sweetly, "would you bring me a candle, a pen, some ink, and some paper?"

Feste's answer was not the one he expected. "Master Malvolio, how did you lose your mind?"

"It is *nonsense* to think I have lost my mind! I have been treated badly, out of ignorance!" shouted Malvolio. "I am not mad any more than you are, Fool!"

"It's always the mad ones who say they are not mad," said Feste.

"I've been shut up in this room. . .in the darkness, by, by. . ."

"By *who*?" asked Feste.

"By those who *hate* me," answered Malvolio. "They lock me up and then send a minister to me. They are doing all they can to make me lose my mind!"

"Calm down," said Feste, "Sir Topas is here." Then Feste began to imitate the minister's voice again. "Malvolio, may you be fortunate, and may heaven make you well."

"Sir Topas! Is that you?" cried Malvolio.

Then Feste, changing his voice again, pretended to say good-by to the minister. "God be with you, Sir Topas," he said.

"Feste, are you there?" asked Malvolio.

"Yes, what do you want?"

"Get me the candle, pen, paper, and ink. I want you to take a letter to my lady for me."

"You are fortunate that I feel sorry for you. I will help you," said Feste.

"Peace to you, Sir," said Malvolio with a sigh. "I will reward you."

*   *   *

Sebastian was standing in Olivia's garden, smiling to himself. *What wonderful air to breathe, what beautiful sunshine,* he thought. He breathed deeply. *I am so happy! I am loved by a beautiful woman! But I wonder what happened to Antonio? I could not find him at The Elephant Inn, where he said to meet him. I wish he were here so he could tell me why I have suddenly become so fortunate. Could I be mad? There's something about all this that I just don't understand.*

Just then, Olivia came walking toward him with a priest. "I know this is quick," she said, "but if you still want to be my husband, come along to the church. I won't be at peace until you are mine. This will be our secret for now. Later, we will tell all our friends. What do you say?"

"I say, YES," replied Sebastian.

Olivia looked at the priest. "Lead the way, good Father, and may heaven shine upon us!"

Help is on the Way

COMPREHENSION CHECK

Choose the best answer.

1. First, Feste puts on a robe and fake beard. Then he goes to Malvolio's room. Next,
____a. Feste sings Malvolio a song.
____b. Toby pretends to be Sir Topas.
____c. Feste brings Malvolio an ink pen.
____d. Feste speaks through the keyhole.

2. Feste
____a. changes his voice to sound like the minister's.
____b. changes his clothes to look like a servant.
____c. asks Olivia to let Malvolio go.
____d. grows a beard to make himself look older.

3. The trick played on Malvolio was done
____a. just for fun.
____b. to get back at Malvolio for being unkind.
____c. to teach Olivia a lesson.
____d. to help Malvolio get over his fear of the dark.

4. Feste, as Sir Topas, calls Malvolio
____a. a fool.
____b. a jolly old fellow.
____c. a madman.
____d. an ignorant man.

5. Malvolio realizes that
____a. no one likes him.
____b. Maria has something to do with all his troubles.
____c. he'll have to speak kindly if he expects to get help.
____d. it's time to quit his job.

6. Malvolio asked Feste for four things. What were they?
____a. Candle, Paper, Pen, and Ink
____b. Candle, Book, Pen, and Ink
____c. Candy, Paper, Pen, and Ink
____d. Candle, Candy, Pen, and Ink

7. Malvolio believes
____a. Olivia is no good.
____b. he is a fortunate man.
____c. he has been set up by those who hate him.
____d. that heaven will make him well.

8. Olivia asks Sebastian to marry her because
____a. she loves Sebastian.
____b. she thinks he's Cesario.
____c. Malvolio turned her down.
____d. she's tired of living alone.

9. Another name for this story could be
____a. "Malvolio Goes Mad!"
____b. "Another Trick!"
____c. "Olivia Goes to Church."
____d. "The Silly Songs of a Fool."

10. This story is mainly about
____a. why Malvolio is afraid of the dark.
____b. why no one likes Malvolio.
____c. three people who have fun at Malvolio's expense (cost).
____d. why Olivia wants to marry Sebastian.

Check your answers with the Key on page 67.

This page may be reproduced for classroom use.

Help is on the Way

VOCABULARY CHECK

breathe	fortunate	imitate	ink	nonsense	robin

I. Sentences to Finish
Fill in the blank in each sentence with the correct key word from the box above.

1. Wouldn't it be great if we could _____ under water?

2. Do you hear that _____ singing in the tree?

3. I feel so _____ to have a good friend like you.

4. I believe ghost stories are nothing but _____.

5. Billy tried to _____ the monkey in the cage by making a monkey face.

6. Peter spilled the blue _____ on Mother's white carpet.

II. Using the Words
On the lines below, write six of your own sentences using the key words from the box above. Use each word once, and draw a circle around the key word.

1. _____

2. _____

3. _____

4. _____

5. _____

6. _____

Check your answers with the Key on page 71.

This page may be reproduced for classroom use.

Brother Finds Sister

PREPARATION

Key Words

especially	(es pesh´ əl ē)	more than usual; particularly *I love ice cream but, I especially like chocolate ice cream.*
explanation	(eks´ plə nā´ shən)	something that explains; a reason *Joey's explanation for being late for class was met with a raised eyebrow.*
favor	(fā´ vər)	a kindness one person does for another *Will you do me a favor and let me borrow your car?*
opposite	(op´ə zit)	a person, thing, or idea that's completely different from another *A good boy is the opposite of a bad boy.* *When I met my blind date, he was the opposite of what I expected.*
service	(sėr´ vis)	help *Our neighbors were a great service to us after our house burned to the ground.*
whom	(hüm)	who; what person; which person *To whom am I speaking?* *Whom do you like best? Steve or Alex?*

Brother Finds Sister

Necessary Words

deceive   (di sēv´)   to make someone believe as true something that is not true; mislead

> *How could you <u>deceive</u> me into thinking this car was a good buy?*
> *Why did you <u>deceive</u> me when you knew I trusted you?*

praise   (prāz)   the act of saying that a thing or person is good; speak well of

> *After she won the Spelling Bee, Mary's uncle called to <u>praise</u> her for a job well done.*

vow   (vou)

1. a serious promise

> *Kyle made a <u>vow</u> to Mary that he would always look after her.*

2. to make a serious promise

> *Patty told Yolanda, "I <u>vow</u> to take good care of your dog while you're away."*

Brother Finds Sister

The Duke asks Feste if he will do him a favor.

Preview: 1. Read the name of the story.
2. Look at the picture.
3. Read the sentence under the picture.
4. Read the first six paragraphs of the story.
5. Then answer the following question.

You learned from your preview that the Duke thought Feste
    ____a. a silly fellow.
    ____b. a clever fellow.
    ____c. a careless fellow.
    ____d. an enemy.

Turn to the Comprehension Check on page 64 for the right answer.

Now read the story.
Read to find out what happens when Sebastian arrives at Olivia's.

Brother Finds Sister

Duke Orsino was tired of hearing about Olivia from Cesario. He wanted to go to her house. When he and Cesario arrived, Feste was in the garden.

"How do you do my good fellow?" asked the Duke.

"The *better* because of my enemies - and the *worse* because of my friends," replied Feste.

"You must mean the opposite," said the Duke.

"Not at all," replied Feste. "My friends praise me and make a fool of me. My enemies tell me plainly that I'm a fool. My enemies do me a favor - while my friends deceive me."

"I praise you because you are especially clever," said the Duke. "Here are some gold coins. If you will do me the favor of telling your lady that I'm here, I'll give you more."

Just then Antonio and the officer appeared.

"Here comes the man who saved me from the duel with Andrew!" said Cesario to the Duke.

The Duke looked at Antonio. "I remember your face. When I last saw you, your ship attacked my ship. I so admired your plan of attack that I thought highly of you."

"This man was in a fight, Sir," said the officer to the Duke.

Cesario spoke next. "This man was very kind to offer to duel with Andrew on my behalf."

"What is your explanation for coming to this place where you have enemies?" the Duke asked Antonio.

Antonio thought Cesario was Sebastian. "I rescued that boy from the sea," he said, pointing to Cesario. "I saved your life, and you talk as though you hardly know me. I've spent every day for the past three months with you. I put myself in danger to watch over you!"

"This man must be mad," Cesario said.

The Duke agreed. "Your words are madness. Just the opposite is true. For the last three months, this boy has been with *me!*"

Just then the Duke saw Olivia and Maria coming toward them. "Now heaven walks on Earth!" he said of Olivia.

"Why have you come here?" Olivia asked the Duke. "If it's about your same old love song, I'm not interested."

"Still so cruel my lady?" replied the Duke. "Since you continue to refuse me, I will take this boy, whom I know you love, away from you. You will never see him again."

To everyone's surprise Cesario said to the Duke, "If that is what you wish, I am ready to go with you."

Thinking Cesario to be her husband, Olivia cried, "Cesario! What are you saying?"

"I am going with the man whom I serve," replied Cesario. "For Duke Orsino, I would a thousand deaths die."

"*Cruel husband!*" Olivia shouted. "How you have deceived me!" She turned to Maria. "*Hurry! Call the priest!*"

Maria continued shouting for some time. Finally, the Duke said, "Come away, Cesario. But, as he started to leave, the priest arrived. "How can I be of service?" he asked Olivia.

"Please tell them what I especially asked you to keep secret," she said.

Pointing to Cesario the priest said, "That man made a vow of love. He is Olivia's husband."

The Duke's eyes opened wide. He turned to Cesario. "You made a vow of love? Why, you have deceived me!" he shouted.

Cesario was about to speak when Andrew and Toby appeared. They both looked like they had been fighting. "I've been hurt!" shouted Andrew. He pointed to Cesario, thinking he was Sebastian. "He cut my head. . . and Toby's too!"

"I *never* hurt you!" shouted Cesario. "You drew your sword for no reason. But I did *nothing* to you."

Olivia could see the men were hurt. "Take them to their beds," she told Maria.

Suddenly, Sebastian appeared! Olivia's face turned white.

"I'm sorry my lady," he said to Olivia. "I have hurt your uncle and his friend. Please forgive me."

Duke Orsino looked at Cesario, then at Sebastian. "One face, one voice, but, *two people!*"

Sebastian saw Antonio. "Antonio! At last!" Then he saw Cesario. He couldn't believe his eyes! "I never had a brother," he began. "I once had a sister, but she drowned."

Viola put two and two together. She gave Sebastian her explanation. "I am your twin sister," she said, letting down her hair. "I didn't drown." Then she told everyone why she had pretended to be a boy.

Orsino looked at the pretty girl before him. "You told me many times that you could never care for a woman as much as you care for me."

"And so I vow again," said Viola.

The Duke smiled. "Your master frees you. For the service you have given me, it would be my pleasure if you would be my wife."

"And a sister to me!" smiled Olivia, taking Sebastian's hand.

Brother Finds Sister

COMPREHENSION CHECK

Choose the best answer.

Preview Answer:
b. a clever fellow.

1. Duke Orsino went to Olivia's
   ___a. to give Feste some gold coins.
   ___b. to bring Olivia some flowers.
   ___c. to praise Olivia.
   ___d. to try to get Olivia to accept his love.

2. First, the Duke and Cesario went to Olivia's where they met Feste in the garden. Then an officer appeared with Antonio. Who appeared in the garden next?
   ___a. Olivia and Maria
   ___b. The priest
   ___c. Sebastian
   ___d. Andrew and Toby

3. Antonio thought Cesario was
   ___a. Viola.
   ___b. Sebastian.
   ___c. Sir Toby.
   ___d. Sir Andrew.

4. Cesario thought Antonio
   ___a. was a great sea captain.
   ___b. was her twin brother.
   ___c. was the man who saved her from a duel with Andrew.
   ___d. was the Duke's enemy.

5. Olivia
   ___a. was happy that the Duke stopped by to see her.
   ___b. was not glad to see the Duke.
   ___c. asked the Duke to leave.
   ___d. was interested to hear what the Duke had to say.

6. Olivia thought
   ___a. Cesario was her husband.
   ___b. her husband was a hard man to get along with.
   ___c. she was losing her mind.
   ___d. the Duke would make some woman very happy.

7. The Duke told Olivia that if she continued to refuse him,
   ___a. she would never be invited to the palace.
   ___b. she would be sorry.
   ___c. she would never see him again.
   ___d. she would never see Cesario again.

8. At the end of the story, both the Duke and Olivia
   ___a. are quite pleased with the way things worked out.
   ___b. can never forgive Viola for what she has done.
   ___c. are sad that there never was a "Cesario."
   ___d. feel that life is not worth living.

9. Another name for this story could be
   ___a. "One Face - One Voice - Two People."
   ___b. "A Vow of Love."
   ___c. "Antonio's Explanation."
   ___d. "Sebastian Finds Antonio."

10. This story is mainly about
    ___a. why Sebastian hurt Andrew and Toby.
    ___b. why Olivia called for the priest.
    ___c. how things worked out for everyone after Viola told her story.
    ___d. Feste's enemies.

Check your answers with the Key on page 67.

This page may be reproduced for classroom use.

Brother finds Sister

VOCABULARY CHECK

especially	explanation	favor	opposite	service	whom

I. Sentences to Finish
Fill in the blank in each sentence with the correct key word from the box above.

1. Alice gave no _____ as to why she quit her job.

2. "For _____ are you buying the gift?" asked the salesman.

3. Sheila did a big _____ for her mother by cleaning the house.

4. Debra wanted to help the poor. *But how can I be of _____? she thought.*

5. Jill does everything well, but she's _____ good at cooking.

6. Mom thought we should head south; Dad thought just the_____, so he headed north.

II. Crossword Puzzle
Use the words from the box above to fill in the puzzle below. Use the meanings below to help you choose the right answer.

Down
1. who; what person; which person
2. more than usual; particularly
4. help

Across
2. reason; something that explains
3. a person, thing, or idea that's completely different from another
5. a kindness one person does for another

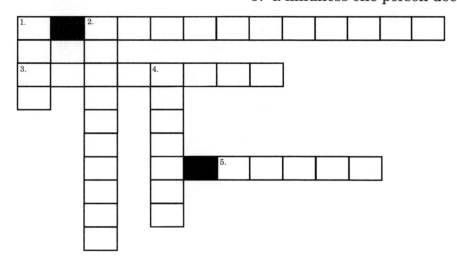

Check your answers with the Key on page 72.

This page may be reproduced for classroom use.

NOTES

COMPREHENSION CHECK ANSWER KEY
Lessons SC 404-31 to SC 404-40

Lesson Number	Question Number										Page Number
	1	2	3	4	5	6	7	8	9	10	
SC-31	c ○	b	c	a	d	b	a	c	b △	d ☐	10
SC-32	c	a	b	d	c ○	a ◇	b ○	b ○	a △	d ☐	16
SC-33	b	c	d	a	a ○	c	b	d ◇	a △	b ☐	22
SC-34	a	c ○	a ○	d	b ○	c ◇	d	a	a △	b ☐	28
SC-35	d	a	c	b ◇	c ○	d	c	a	a △	c ☐	34
SC-36	c	d ○	a	a	b	c ○	b ◇	d ○	c △	a ☐	40
SC-37	c	d	a	b ○	c	c	a ◇	b ○	c △	d ☐	46
SC-38	a	c	b	d	a	b ○	c ◇	d	b △	a ☐	52
SC-39	d ◇	a	b ○	c	c	a	c	b ○	b △	c ☐	58
SC-30	d ○	a ◇	b	c	b ○	a	d	a ○	a △	c ☐	64

○ = Inference (not said straight out, but you know from what is said)

△ = Another name for the story

☐ = Main idea of the story

◇ = Sequence (recalling order of events in the story)

NOTES

VOCABULARY CHECK ANSWER KEY
Lessons SC 404-31 to SC 404-33

LESSON NUMBER   **PAGE NUMBER**

31   ARRIVAL IN ILLYRIA   11

I.		*II.*	
1.	instrument	1.	e
2.	music	2.	c
3.	shone	3.	d
4.	coin	4.	b
5.	helpful	5.	a
6.	mast	6.	f

32   FALLING IN LOVE   17

I.		*II.*	
1.	manners	1.	NO
2.	jealous	2.	NO
3.	burst	3.	YES
4.	gentleman	4.	NO
5.	favorite	5.	YES
6.	entire	6.	NO

33   COMINGS AND GOINGS   23

I.	
1.	midnight
2.	sight
3.	fond
4.	flute
5.	companion
6.	couple

VOCABULARY CHECK ANSWER KEY
Lessons SC 404-34 to SC 404-36

LESSON NUMBER

PAGE NUMBER

34 **SECRETS AND TRICKS** **29**

I.
1. disappointment
2. seal
3. stocking
4. accept
5. command
6. crouch

II.
1. NO
2. NO
3. YES
4. YES
5. NO
6. NO

35 **PRETENDING BRINGS TROUBLE** **35**

I.
1. God
2. admire
3. bet
4. coax
5. Although
6. dull

II.

```
A  D  M  I  R  E  X  E
C  U  O  G  O  B  C  L
O  L  D  U  L  E  O  T
A  L  T  H  O  U  G  H
X  U  X  A  D  M  O  O
S  I  T  B  E  T  D  S
```

36 **MALVOLIO IS MADE THE FOOL** **41**

I.
1. grateful
2. hadn't
3. property
4. port
5. arrest
6. explore

II.
1. a
2. a
3. b
4. b
5. b
6. a

VOCABULARY CHECK ANSWER KEY
Lessons SC 404-37 to SC 404-39

LESSON NUMBER		PAGE NUMBER

37   DRAWING SWORDS   47

I.   1. treat   *II.* 1. contain
    2. dignity   2. thankful
    3. thankful   3. dignity
    4. contain   4. habit
    5. habit   5. lad
    6. lad   6. treat
                        Hidden Word: Fabian

38   THE STRUGGLE   53

I.   1. mystery   *II.* 1. b
    2. remove   2. a
    3. ache   3. b
    4. nuisance   4. b
    5. shoulder   5. b
    6. Quit   6. b

39   HELP IS ON THE WAY   59

I.   1. breathe
    2. robin
    3. fortunate
    4. nonsense
    5. imitate
    6. ink

VOCABULARY CHECK ANSWER KEY
LESSON SC 404-40

LESSON NUMBER		PAGE NUMBER

40   BROTHER FINDS SISTER   **65**

I.   1. explanation
      2. whom
      3. favor
      4. service
      5. especially
      6. opposite

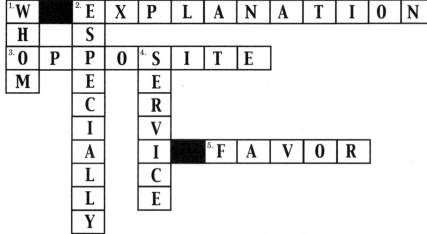